FROM THE FRYING PAN INTO THE FIRE

Memoir of a Zimbabwean

Judith Mawoko

◆ FriesenPress

Suite 300 - 990 Fort St
Victoria, BC, V8V 3K2
Canada

www.friesenpress.com

Copyright © 2018 by Judith Mawoko
First Edition — 2018

ISBN
978-1-5255-2260-4 (Hardcover)
978-1-5255-2261-1 (Paperback)
978-1-5255-2262-8 (eBook)

1. BIOGRAPHY & AUTOBIOGRAPHY, CULTURAL HERITAGE

Distributed to the trade by The Ingram Book Company

TABLE OF CONTENTS

In memory of Mom and Dad,
and my siblings Cybert and Agnes,
who are sadly missed.

COW FOOT IN COWPEAS

My memories go back to 1972 when I was sent to live with my maternal grandmother, Mbuya Kasipo, in Rupinda village. It was a five hour walk from my village, but with my small feet it felt like we walked for eternity. I was seven years old and going to start school. I did my Grade 1 at Costern School, which was perched at the summit of a mountain, bordering Rhodesia and Portuguese East Africa (now Zimbabwe and Mozambique). The school was a good two hour walk from home.

I remember my grandmother for her storytelling skill. Every night after supper we gathered around her to listen to folk tales that she told with so much zeal that she could make us laugh and cry at the same time.

I also remember her for her cooking. She made the most savoury dishes. One of her favorite recipes was cow foot mixed with cowpeas (*mazondo munyemba*). It was a delicious mix. My favourite part of the mix was of course mazondo, the meat part.

One day, I came home from school and found my grandmother working in the field just behind the cooking hut. She told me that she had prepared this famous dish and that I could go in and serve myself. I just needed to leave enough food for my cousins, Lovemore and Violet, who were in upper grades and had stayed in school for sports that afternoon.

I went inside the hut and found the familiar clay pot sitting on the open fireplace in the centre of the hut. The fire had since died down. The tantalizing aroma of the delicious dish filled the air. I was salivating as I picked out a wooden plate and spoon to serve myself.

My first scoop yielded only *nyemba,* no mazondo. The second and third scoops produced the same result, and I began to wonder whether Mbuya had forgotten to cook the cow foot, so I went out to inquire.

"*Mbuya, hamuna nyama umu!* Grandma, there is no meat in here!" I yelled.

My grandmother yelled back *"Haa wakapusa iwe poto izere mazondo iyo!* You're stupid, that pot is full of cow foot!"

I went back inside totally confused. I held back my tears as I gobbled down the cowpeas, very disappointed and angry that Mbuya had lied to me about mazondo, and was still insisting upon it. It wasn't a funny joke.

When I was full of nyemba I joined Grandma in the field, not daring to mention that topic again.

Then came my cousins from school, and they were told the same thing: to go inside and serve themselves the delicious cuisine.

I watched them with curiosity and anxiety as they entered the hut. Then Lovemore immediately came back out to make the same complaint that I had made earlier, *"Mbuya, hamuna nyama umu!"*

Then it dawned on Mbuya that something must be wrong. She went inside to check for herself, and for sure there was no trace of cow foot in there, only cowpeas.

We all stood outside the hut, arms crossed, totally puzzled by the mystery of the vanished cow foot.

Right next to the cooking hut was the grain storage room, a small four-cornered hut balancing on rock stilts. Just then, Bhoki emerged from the base of this structure, licking his snout and happily wagging his tail. Behind him was a trail of bones.

My grandmother's name was Judith. I was named after her. I don't know the exact year of my grandmother's birth, but considering that my mom was born 1939, and that she had two older siblings, I can assume that Grandmother was born around 1915. You may wonder why my grandmother had such a European name. That's because when European missionaries came to southern Africa in the mid-nineteenth century, they preached that any traditional forms of worshiping God were barbaric and primitive, and African names were ungodly. Therefore it became the fashionable and civilized thing for parents to give their babies European names. Thus, my grandmother got the name Judith, and in turn, she gave all her children European names. Naomi, Victor, Laura, and Margaret. Only that all the names got a Shona twist: Judisi, Naume, Vikita, Rora and Megi.

When I lived with my grandmother, my grandfather was there too, but he was not part of us. He had married a second wife, much younger than my grandmother, and she had two young sons. We were not allowed to play with his kids or even to talk to his wife. My grandfather lived with them in a separate set of huts just a few metres away from ours, but we never interacted with them. I don't remember talking to my grandpa at all. We just met him out there while we were out herding cattle or goats, or collecting water or firewood.

I later learnt that I had been sent to stay with my grandmother because of ill-health. I was failing to thrive. I was always sneezing, coughing and passing diarrhoea. Sometimes I threw up all day. The clinic was two hours away, across a river, which flooded in the rainy season. My grandmother had a good knowledge of herbal medicines, which she mixed in her nutritious dishes such as *mazondo munyemba*. Although I was never diagnosed with a major disease, I believe my grandmother might have cured me of a disease that was going undiagnosed and could have killed me. Whatever she put into those herbal concoctions worked in my favour. Since then I've enjoyed a very healthy life.

Mbuya was in fact the doctor of the entire village and beyond. People came to her with all manner of ailments. I remember one neighbour who suddenly burst into our hut with an emergency. He held a screaming child with severe burns. Boiling water had peeled the skin off his entire face and neck. That freaked me out, but my grandma was undaunted by it. She quickly scooped him off his father's arms and set to work on him.

She was also an expert midwife. Pregnant women were brought to our home to deliver their babies. By the time the babies left, they had received several doses of herbal concoctions she prepared for them to build their immune systems.

She had a separate hut designated for medical purposes. She used to take me out into the bush to dig up roots and to collect some buds and leaves. By the time I left I knew quite a few herbal remedies.

There was no charge for her services. A satisfied patient just brought a token of appreciation: a hen, a goat, a headscarf or anything they could afford.

White people had coined the term witch doctors, to refer to traditional healers like my grandma. The word witch has the connotations of evil and malice, the very opposite of what my grandmother did for her people.

TRANQUILITY

I was returned to my mother for my second grade. It was nice to be reunited with my family. At that age of eight, I had three older siblings and three younger ones aged six, four, and two, and Mom was pregnant. It was a full house indeed.

From the day I returned home there was one particular sibling who caught my attention. She had a more vibrant personality than mine in every respect. I smiled. She laughed. I walked. She ran. I chewed my food. She gobbled down hers. She was taller and stronger. She was faster.

She was naughtier. She was everything that I was not. She wondered where I fit in the family. If I was older than her, then why was I so much smaller? So she convinced herself that they must be joking. She was older. We fought battles for seniority throughout our early childhood.

When I was eight, going for Grade 2, she was six. The requirement was for all black children to turn seven before starting school, based on the assumption that black children were genetically incapable of handling formal education so early. So my sister needed to wait another year, but she wouldn't hear of it. She woke up before me on the first day of school. She had eaten her breakfast and was ready to go before I was. There was no leaving her behind, so Mom just let her go with me, assuming that she would be turned back. When we arrived at school she stuck with me like a leech. She spent the day with me in Grade 2, answering the roll call when my name was called, sitting on my spot, and collecting the books and pencils that were meant for me. The Grade 2 teacher, who was also the headmaster, Mr. Mbona, didn't mind her at all. He was just being entertained. After a few days he convinced her to go to Grade 1 instead. That's how Agnes ended up being just a year behind me throughout elementary school.

Every morning before school, each child had to do some household chores so we had to get up early. No one had a watch or clock to tell the time. We relied on cocks, whose cock-a doodle-doos always came at the exact same time every morning before daybreak. These roosters performed the daily duty of alerting us of dawn with an accurate timing that never failed.

We had to go to the well to fetch fresh drinking water in buckets. Our parents advised us not to drink stagnant water from puddles, or running water from small streams around us. Our teachers taught us about germs and hookworms that could cause serious diseases. There were lots of natural springs around us. The water table in our village was very high so we did not have to go too far, or to dig too deep to get a clean water supply. No purification chemicals were necessary. This water had already been naturally purified by osmosis.

We also had to make a fire at the centre of the cooking hut. By the time we started school we were experts at starting a fire safely. Then we had to warm up some water to wash our faces, arms and legs. A full bath would have to wait for the weekend when we could bathe in the river.

We then made tea. There was always the luxury of plenty of milk in the tea. We always had one or two cows to milk. To accompany the tea cup we had sweet potatoes, pumpkins, yams and sometimes cornmeal left over from the night's supper. After that we changed into our blue school uniform tunics if we had them. Boys wore khaki shirts and shorts. If anybody could not afford the school uniform, our teachers did not make a big deal about it. We all had to shave our heads, both boys and girls, or keep the hair very short. Once that was all good we were ready to leave. On the way to school we would break small twigs from the Muhacha tree. We chewed up one end resemble bristles of a toothbrush, and brushed our teeth as we walked to school. That was enough to keep our teeth white and to prevent tooth decay.

Our school was just a twenty minute walk from home. That is if we were walking leisurely and picking up our friends along the way.

Morning assembly was held right under the sky, in front of the headmaster's Grade 2 classroom, which was also his office. We lined up by grade level. There was dead silence. You could hear a pin drop. We all opened our mouths as wide as we could, baring our teeth. If you were a foreigner arriving in this scenario you might have become a little suspicious and scared, but no we were not going to bite you. We were just displaying our teeth for inspection. We also had our arms extended and fingers bent to show our fingernails. Our teachers also inspected our hair. Dirty teeth, long fingernails, and unkempt hair were punishable offences. Those who arrived late joined the rank of offenders.

We had to bend down and touch our toes. Then we got two or three hard lashes on our buttocks with a cane. If we were lucky, our teachers had their blackboard dusters ready to give us a few merciless knocks on our knuckles. The natural response was to jump up and down, shaking our hands and licking our knuckles to alleviate the pain. Then we would run into the nearby bushes to get thorny twigs to brush our hair, break twigs to use as toothbrushes, then find a rock to scratch until the overgrown nails evened out. That was all done in a flash because another five minutes lateness would invite a fresh ordeal. From the assembly point we marched single file, military style, in different directions to our respective classrooms, which were scattered haphazardly on that hilly, rocky landscape.

Other than that, school was fun. I was very bright and grasped the concepts fast. We had five teachers. Besides the headmaster, there was Mr. Mukasi and his wife, Madame Mukasi, then we had Mr. Gwete, and Mr. Mupeti, who was my favourite teacher. Oh yes, we still loved our teachers even though they knocked our knuckles with blackboard dusters. We never regarded that as abuse. In fact, that word was unknown to us. They were loving teachers who just wanted to make the best out of us and our parents respected them highly.

Mr. Mupeti performed wonders in the classroom to make learning fun. His sense of humour was unsurpassed and his creativity was remarkable. He arranged our science field trips, no bus necessary, and no parent consent forms required. We just spread out into the thick bush behind our school to find animals in their natural habitats.

We scared a myriad of birds out of their nests: sparrows, weavers, hornbills, and sunbirds. One little skittish robin was too reluctant to leave its nest unattended. It perched itself in a nearby branch and shrieked frantically. We were not interested in its little miserable looking, featherless chicks that lay helplessly in the nest with beaks wide open, waiting for Mama to drop in a worm or a nut.

We were more fascinated with the green mamba that slithered up the tree to ambush a chameleon basking in the sun, but the chameleon, with its swivelling eyes, had noticed it first. It intimidated the predator with rapid colour changes, displaying dazzling arrays of red, yellow, green and white. The confused snake turned to raid the little robin's nest instead.

We startled a huge tortoise, to hide in its shell. A hare suddenly sprang out of the bush and darted away. We dug out a rat but it shot out of the hole and vanished in the dense brown undergrowth. Meanwhile, there was a troop of monkeys swinging in the high branches. It looked like they were teasing and challenging us to a race as they chattered along, glancing down at us every now and then. Some of us decided to take up the challenge and started to climb up the trees. They were distracted from the lesson.

"Stop that monkey business!" yelled our teacher.

Just then, my friend Hudson suddenly let go of the branch he was hanging on and landed with a thud, rolling on the ground and waving his arms wildly around his head in pain and panic. Apparently, he had disturbed a nest of wasps and they had come out for him in fury. He went home with bulging eyes and dangling lips, but that was no big deal. We were immune to bug bites. There was no such thing as allergies. We had never heard of that word. We teased him about the funny swellings he got from the mean little stingers. They made him look like an alien from space. Bug bites were a daily occurrence. Everybody got stung by a bee, wasp, ant or mosquito on a regular basis so this was nothing unusual.

Our teacher blew the whistle and we instantly gathered around him for a quick summary of our lesson before we returned to school.

The major parts of the curriculum were literacy and numeracy. Then there was the content subject, which was a mix of history, geography, and science. The whole curriculum was taught in English, which we were encouraged to speak in the classroom. Outside the classroom and at home we spoke our Shona language, which we were also learning to read and write. My favourite part was when we went out to practice printing, in the sand, or to collect pebbles or sticks to use as manipulatives for math.

Our worst subject was history. We memorised facts about the European explorers, Ferdinand Magellan, Christopher Columbus, Vasco da Gama, Jacques Cartier, Cecil John Rhodes, David Livingston and many others. We always got the names mixed up. The dates were hard to remember and the concept of a world map was too abstract for us. Our world was bounded by the mountains that surrounded us.

We didn't have any library books but our textbooks had enough reading materials to enable us to master the English language, particularly the reading and writing skills. We also had a radio lesson, in which a native speaker of the English language delivered a lesson for each grade level over the radio, for half an hour. That was intended to expose us to the proper standard of spoken English. We were supposed to tune in to the relevant radio station at the time scheduled for our grade level, but we usually missed part of the radio lesson since we had one tiny wireless radio for the whole school. After the lesson a student had to zip across the school yard to the next classroom block to deliver the little gadget. One rainy day when it was my turn to do the delivery I suddenly slipped and fell, in the mud puddle, sending the little appliance spinning in the air. By the time I picked myself up and completed the delivery, half the listening lesson had been delivered to the sparrows and squirrels out there.

Since our school was located at the foot of a large mountain, sometimes we lost the radio signal, and the sound faded into a continuous buzz. This technological glitch happened quite often, so we missed many of the lessons.

In our Grade 4 radio lesson I remember listening to the reading of H. Rider Haggard's book, *King Solomon's Mines*. We marvelled at how the civilized and superior

European characters played tricks on the primitive and ignorant Africans, who were superstitious.

During our Shona lessons we had the opportunity to listen to our teachers read novels written in our own language by indigenous authors. Shona novels were always a treat. They resonated with our everyday life style.

In the afternoons we did handicrafts. We collected a certain kind of fine clay from the stream banks, and used it to mold clay pots or to make our toy cows, goats and dogs. We also made bamboo baskets and mats. Boys learnt to carve soapstone sculptures, and to make wooden gadgets such as cooking sticks and hoe handles.

We also had sports in the afternoons, soccer for boys and netball for girls. We held tournaments with neighbouring schools. My brother Justin was in the soccer team. I never played sports myself. I just didn't have the stamina for it, but my favourite part was cheering for our teams. That was a contest on its own. We danced and sang loudly to stifle the sound from the opposing team's supporters, while they tried to do the same. At the end of it, it sounded like a swarm of bees had descended upon the land. In the brutal heat of Africa we would be totally drenched in our own perspiration, which gave our skins a glossy look and sticky feel. We were sweating more profusely than the players, and covered in dust from head to toe. It was hilarious.

We brought our own refreshments from home. Depending on the season, we had sugarcane, fresh corn on the cob, or previously dried corn (*mangai*) popcorn, bananas, mangoes, guavas as well as wild fruit for which there are no English names: *nhengeni, matunduru, mazhanje, tsubvu, tsombori,* and *nhunguru.* No one went hungry. We cared and we shared.

We were not allowed to bring our food into the classrooms for fear of inviting cockroaches and rats. So we had to hide our food in the bushes surrounding the school. By lunch time our corn on the cob was slimy from the hot sun, and it was infested with ants, spiders, snails and other creepy crawlies. We simply shook them off and munched on our food.

We all walked to and from school. The only vehicle in the community belonged to the headmaster Mr. Mbona. Each time that little Daihatsu pickup truck passed us playing on the narrow, potholed dusty road, we always abandoned our games to chase it, huffing and puffing in the cloud of dust that totally enshrouded us, leaving us gasping for breath. We could never catch up with the car but that did not stop us trying.

On the way home from school sometimes there was boxing entertainment. Our school served two villages, the Duri village to the east and the Kwambana village to the west. The school was the boundary. There was a perpetual feud between boys from the two villages. These boys were not tiny tots. Although the official age to start school was seven years, some parents who did not care much about school did not enrol their kids until they were nine or ten. Other kids repeated grades multiple times. So it was not surprising to find teenagers as old as fifteen, in fifth grade.

The big boys from the two villages sometimes challenged each other to fist fights in the sand, in the dry river bed.

Word would spread quickly around the school, that there would be a game in the sand that afternoon. Everyone knew what that meant. Teachers were not supposed to know this, so it was top secret. After dismissal we would converge at the river bed.

One day there was a big fight between Shakespeare and Duru. The fight instigator initiated the game by making two heaps of sand. Each opponent knew that the sand heap made closest to him represented his mother's boob. Shakespeare, who was the challenger, dared the reigning champion by kicking his sand heap. That infuriated his opponent and the duel began.

"How dare you kick my mother's boob!" shouted Duru as he flared in anger. They started pelting each other with fists. Blows rained in all directions, much to the delight of the jubilant spectators.

They would not kill each other. There was always the good-natured referee who would throw in the towel after a few bruises and a nosebleed. Sometimes an adult just happened by, and we would scatter and hide in the bushes. Nobody wanted their parents to know that they were part of this roguish behaviour.

In the bushes we ate wild fruit. We were advised not to be wasteful because we needed to share the fruit with wild animals, so we took only what we needed. Sometimes we just climbed up the trees to swing on the branches, with monkeys, squirrels, lizards, and all kinds of birds. Nobody ever got bitten by a snake although there were plenty of them, because they ran from us, and we ran from them. There was always that mutual respect between us, or mutual fear. We were advised that all snakes were venomous, regardless of their types or sizes. So nobody ever dared to go near a snake.

We roamed everywhere we wanted, but there was one place we dared not go. That was the village cemetery. That just scared us to death. The cemetery was in a thick forest behind the church. People never went there except for funerals, which were very rare. So there were very old tall trees and an undergrowth of thick bushes and tall grass. I was so freaked out by this place that each time I passed by it I would hold my breath and bolt past at lightning speed.

One day, Mr. Mupeti decided to demystify the graveyard for us. We were learning about decomposition. "For our next science project we are going into the cemetery," he announced.

There was dead silence. I looked around to see if everyone else had heard what I heard. They were all passing similar glances at one another. Then we all looked at Mr. Mupeti with questioning looks. Was he going cuckoo?

"Yes, you all heard me right, the graveyard," he said.

We were going to make compost heaps using dead leaves. The cemetery was the best place to collect the leaves because there was not much human activity in there so there were layers upon layers of leaves that were already in the process of decay. They would decompose a lot faster if we speeded up the process a little, by covering our compost heaps with soil and watering them every day.

So we all made our solemn procession into the cemetery, to collect leaves.

It was solemn indeed as we trudged through the dense dry grass in total silence, twenty-six kids in single file, led by Teacher Mupeti. It was tense. The only whisper we could hear was the crunchy, crackling sound of the dead leaves as we shuffled through them, deeper into the forest. The graves were just heaps of rocks. A few had been marked with cement slabs. They were all almost covered with leaves and weeds.

The only person who was totally untroubled by this atmosphere was Mr. Mupeti. He was rattling on and on, even cracking jokes.

"Hey guys! Why are dead people buried in a cemetery?" he asked.

There was silence.

"Any takers?" he asked again. He was just enjoying himself. Again there was no response.

"Because they are dead people!" he beamed, laughing at his own joke. Nobody said anything. Was he really expecting us to laugh in a cemetery?

He even sat on a grave and told us to gather around him for a little lecture about decomposition. He said that when people die, their bodies decompose and over a long period even their bones turn into dust. So in some of these old graves, there was nothing but dust.

We then filled up our burlap sacks with leaves and filed back to school, surprised that we hadn't seen any ghostly apparitions. We hadn't heard any eerie murmurs or guttural sounds from people of the underworld. All that we had heard was the ubiquitous chirping of birds and the ear-piercing shrills of cicadas that we heard in any other forest. There was a lot of interesting wildlife in that cemetery if we had cared to look around us, instead of staring at the rocky mounds, expecting the dust to turn into malicious goblins that would assail us. The next time I passed by the cemetery I walked by leisurely.

I've heard it said, that there are some people who are teachers, and then there are others, who are educators. It is true.

Our school was beautiful. It was a set of three rectangular brick buildings, with whitewashed walls inside and out. They were roofed with corrugated iron sheets. There were wooden tables and chairs inside, enough furniture for thirty students in each. To the north end of the classroom blocks was the best building of them all, the Anglican church. The school had been established by Anglican missionaries.

To the south, in the windward direction, and isolated from the rest of the buildings, was another rectangular whitewashed building, but this was a little different. It was very narrow, maybe just two metres wide, and it had no windows, just small triangular holes up there. It was also not as tall as the other buildings. An adult would have to bend down a little to enter it. If you were viewing this structure from the classroom blocks, it would seem as if it had no door. But it actually had a door facing away from the rest of the buildings. A foreigner to the land would be a little puzzled and would move closer to investigate, but would soon be smacked in the face by the repelling, nauseating stench that exuded from that building. It would force him to make a sudden U-turn.

This pit latrine was one long block with a wall to separate boys from girls. Inside was a concrete floor. There was a row of six small triangular holes, small enough for a little child to squat with legs astride it. Needless to say it was very common for children to miss the tiny squat holes and mess up the floor. Flies loved that. Under the concrete floor was a very deep pit measuring about the same length and width as the building, and three to four metres deep.

There was no fence around the school, so when the children went home, cows and goats were at liberty to bring their friends and families to forage around the buildings. People watched their livestock closely during the farming season to prevent them from destroying crops, but during the dry season they just let them loose during the day and collected them for the night.

No child ever fell into the school toilet. Oops, actually a kid did fall into the toilet.

One afternoon when we came back to look for our animals we witnessed a mother of a different species frantically circling the toilet block.

"Maa! Maa!" she cried as she trotted clockwise and counter-clockwise repeatedly as if she was chasing something invisible to us. Naturally, our curiosity kicked in so we drew closer to investigate. The answer to our curiosity came from inside the latrine.

"Maaaa! Maaaa! Maaaa!" came the high-pitched, distant, desperate cry of a very young kid. The impatient mother goat probably thought her kid was playing the silly game of catch-me-if-you-can, around the building. Little did she know that her curious little darling had been lured into the toilet by the smell of urine. She had been swallowed by that beast of a toilet and was calling from deep down its gut.

There was no way to retrieve a little baby goat from that disgusting shit down there. The next day the kid had stopped bleating and its grieving mother was gone. She had learnt her lesson the hard way, not to bring underage kids to this school.

During the farming season, it was our job to look after cattle and goats after school. We were dismissed from school at one o'clock every day except on sports days, so we spent the rest of the afternoon in the pastures along the river bank or up the hills. We enjoyed climbing up tall trees, playing hide and seek in the bushes and collecting fruits, edible herbs and berries.

Quite often, we would provoke bulls to fight each other. Bulls are very territorial and aggressive, and will fight for dominance, so we were supposed to avoid mixing bulls that were unacquainted to each other, because that would automatically instigate a fight, but we did it anyway. It was always thrilling to watch two ferocious beasts charging at each other and locking their massive horns in nerve-wracking combats that could last for an hour. Sometimes we got so absorbed in watching bull fights that we did not notice the other animals straying away into fields and destroying crops. That offence was always punishable by spanking. To reduce the aggressive behaviour of the bulls people castrated most of them, leaving only a few for breeding purposes.

Every day had its own adventures. There was never a dull moment. There was no boredom, no loneliness, and no stress. The word poverty was unknown to us. What was poverty? Our grain storage rooms were full of corn. We had livestock. We went to school. We had friends. We had loving parents and countless aunts, uncles and cousins. We had roofs above our heads to protect us from the rain. We had no worries, no problems.

Sliding was a regular pastime in the dry season. We had our sliding slope conveniently located in the small brook that ran through our village. That is where we also took our baths and did our laundry. The slide was a smooth rock surface slopping gently downstream, probably seventy metres long. In the dry season there was a trickle of water flowing through it, just the right amount to create a perfect world class natural slide for us. We just sat on our bare butts at the top of the slide, and plunged down the slope into the puddle below. For extra speed we rubbed soap suds onto our butts, then we would zip down pretty fast. One day our friend Idah suddenly lost balance and flipped over. She tumbled down unceremoniously, landing in the puddle with a nasty thud. The water quickly turned red. Her cheek had split open all the way from the mouth to the ear. She didn't cry and nobody panicked. Her mom bundled her up and walked the five kilometres to the nearest clinic to get her cheek stitched up.

For swimming, we went down to the Honde River. We never swam in it during the rainy season because it often flooded and there was the high risk of drowning, but in the dry season it was safe. Because of the sandy river bed the water was very clear. Smaller kids spent their time splashing in the shallow puddles, learning to swim. Those who had mastered the skill went further downstream to a deep blue pool called *Rufairi* (Raphael). So-called because a child by that name had drowned in that pool a generation before. At Rufairi we all stripped naked, both boys and girls. Nobody seemed to notice our nudity and nobody was uneasy about it. We even had a natural diving board, a huge boulder hanging over the pool. Nobody knew how deep that pool was or what lay beneath it, but we just plunged in.

We climbed real mountains. The forest provided free firewood and herbal medicine. It also yielded abundant fruit. The sun shone upon us every day without fail and the moonlight turned night into day, giving us extended hours to play outside.

The weather was warm enough for birds to sing sweetly in the trees all year round. Crickets and grasshoppers chirped in the meadows. Monkeys chattered and baboons barked in the mountains. Hyenas laughed, and owls hooted, punctuating the night's silence. Cocks crowed in the mornings. Life was good.

Occasionally, there was a wedding. It was always a mixture of traditional marriage rituals and the blessing of the marriage by the Anglican priest. The bride price of a few cows and goats would have been paid prior to the event, and it was time to hand over the bride to the new family.

It was fun fare throughout the day. One memorable wedding was that of Prisca and John.

Early in the morning, we all converged in the church for the official solemnization of the wedding by a white priest, Father Woodrow, who had driven his Land Rover two hours from St. Augustine's Mission, for this event. John wore a black suit. Prisca had a long white gown, nothing fancy but she looked angelic in it. They repeated their vows the usual Anglican way. From church they walked home, with a whole train of people following them, singing and dancing. The official wedding reception was right under the blazing sun outside the cooking hut. The wedding party got the privilege to sit in the shade of the big mango tree in front of the hut. A small table had been set up for them, big enough for four people. They had a train of wedding maids too. They all wore blue homemade cotton dresses. Whoever made them did a rough job indeed, but nobody cared. What they wore on their feet didn't matter. Some had Bata flip flops that shovelled up the sand. Others had black rubber sandals that looked something like what we call Crocs today. In those days we called them Sandak. Some had faded, worn out canvas shoes, in all the different colours of the rainbow. None of them was barefoot. So that was awesome.

While people poured into the homestead, our renowned drummer Lameck took his stand behind the African drum. He beat it with a passion. It rumbled, making the earth vibrate under our feet. The thunderous booms reverberated across the mountains surrounding us, inviting more people from far and wide. Everyone was welcome.

Meanwhile, volunteers were preparing the big feast. They slaughtered and butchered a cow early in the morning. They made a big fire. Three big boulders were used to make a tripod stand on which they balanced a giant metal barrel to use as the pot. The recipe was simple:

† Chop up the whole cow including its head and feet.

† Boil it forever.

† Add salt, and serve.

The accompaniment for this dish was the usual maize meal (*sadza*). Because it was prepared in bulk, on a big fire, this sadza always assumed a burnt flavour, but that was tolerable at a wedding.

Plates were served at the high table, but for the rest of the multitude, plates were not necessary. The plate-shaped leaves of the *Muzhanje* tree served the purpose well. Kids rushed into the bush to prune off the leaves, which they spread on the ground in the middle of groups of people. Then the waiters came along, dropping huge mounds of sadza and the meat, and we dug in.

After the food it was time for the wedding gifts, and our distinguished announcer Killer, took his stand. Killer was not a murderer by the way. That's the English name his parents gave him just because it sounded cute. They obviously didn't know what that word meant. Anyway Killer had a prominent voice that could be heard from across the river. He stood on a log platform and people handed him their presents to announce. He received a penny or two, a little red hen, or a scrawny little goat, an axe or a hoe, a basket or a bamboo mat, a clay pot or some other household item. People cheered, clapped and whistled after each gift was announced.

After the wedding gifts, we went back to the drumming and dancing. The resonant, energizing, thunderous rhythm of the drum was irresistible. There were no spectators. Everyone was a performer. We twirled, twisted and twerked. We scuttled and shuffled. We swayed and spun. We tiptoed and trotted, clapped and crawled. We whistled and ululated. Everyone was possessed by the spirit of joy. We raised a cloud of dust until sunset.

Call me nostalgic, but life was good indeed.

Sometimes, in the dead of night we heard the distant roar of a lion. Nobody ever claimed to have seen one in person. We were advised to stay away from the mountain at night and not to penetrate into its deeper crevices during the day, and we obeyed. We respected large predator animals' privacy and they respected ours.

One night, there was a commotion inside our cattle pens. Bulls were bellowing wildly. Then we heard the howl of a hyena. Men rushed out to the rescue with sticks and spears. The hyenas escaped. We did not lose any of our beasts but in the morning we noticed that several cows had had their tails nipped right off.

Once in a while there was the occasional snake that accidentally slithered into a hut while chasing a rat. That one got the maximum sentence for intruding on us. We made sure that it did not leave that hut whole. We thrashed it to pieces and threw the remains in a hell of fire.

There was gossip about witches in the village. These were ordinary people who, supposedly, transformed into some invisible forms at night. They were then able to ride on hyenas, cats or owls, mysteriously entering locked doors while people were sleeping. They were believed to cause all manner of ailments, bad luck, and death. They could even enter sealed graves to eat the dead bodies. Usually, the prime suspects for this kind of behaviour were the little wrinkled old men and women who staggered along with walking sticks.

I always questioned the logic of it all. If they were bad people at night how come they were so nice during the day? They greeted and smiled, like everyone else. They offered others food, and they worked as hard as everyone else to produce from the soil. So what did they benefit from their nighttime endeavours?

In those days, I remember only one death in the community, that of an old man who had suffered from leprosy. Other than that, new babies were born, toddlers grew up, children went to school, young men and women got married, and the cycle of life repeated itself.

When a new baby was born we always had a big celebration. People converged to congratulate the new parents, and brought gifts. We did not celebrate birthdays annually though. Our whole lifestyle was a continuous celebration of life.

For Saturdays, women brewed millet beer for their husbands. The men would all go from household to household to share their special treat. They all drank from the same beer mug that they passed from one person to another. Nobody ever got sick from that, even though most of them never brushed their teeth and they dipped their dirty long moustaches in the beer.

My mom used to brew beer too, when our dad was coming for Christmas. Women in our village did not drink or smoke. They were not forbidden. It was just the norm. Men made their own cigarettes by simply wrapping dried tobacco in newspaper. Then they dragged the thick black smoke that left their teeth as black as charcoal. My dad was a town guy so he bought Madison cigarettes, but he always brought enough to share with others.

The drinking parties were very noisy occasions, but there was no fighting. All the energy was taken up with drumming, singing, dancing and laughing.

Sometimes men had hunting parties. They went into the bushes with dogs and wooden clubs that they used as weapons to knock down small animals like rabbits and deer, and then they would butcher their catch and share the meat at the end of the day.

The usual outfit for men was blue coveralls. They manufactured their own sandals from old car tires. Everyone dressed simply. Even those who worked in the cities blended with those in the village by dressing like them when they came home for weekends.

Women usually had work parties in the fields. They would all spend a day on one person's field, singing and chatting together while weeding or harvesting the crop. The next day, they would go to another field until all the work was done. Nobody was ever left alone. If anyone was unable to work because of illness, their crop did not go to waste. All women would choose a day to get that work done. Men did the harder work of ploughing the land with ox-drawn ploughs. They were also responsible for cutting down trees for firewood, and building huts.

Our home was the envy of the neighbourhood. We slept in an L-shaped house, with three rooms and a veranda. It had brick walls, and instead of the regular grass thatch that everyone else had, we had a corrugated iron sheet roof. Facing the house was the regular grass thatched, round hut, with a fireplace in the centre. That was our kitchen and living room. The grass roof kept the room cool. Smoke filtered out through the roof so it never accumulated inside the hut. Next to the kitchen was a smaller hut, which was the grain storage room. A little removed from this cluster of buildings was our tiny pit latrine. All buildings were painted yellow, which made our homestead stand out in the whole neighbourhood.

This was so because we had a father working for the national railways company, Rhodesia Railways. He was a clerk. His name was Nathan Taengwa Mawoko. Dad did not make a lot of money but he was able to send enough money home for my mother to hire a fairly good builder to construct some decent structures with bricks. He also bought cement, to make concrete floors, and he bought the corrugated iron sheets for the roof. Dad also sent enough money for us all to get at least one special dress and canvas shoes for Sundays. We also had one school uniform each, and a few other old hand-me-down clothes that were passed from the older kids to the younger ones.

During the dry season, when mom was not growing crops, she used to take us to the capital city of Salisbury to our dad during the August school holidays. In Salisbury, he had a four-roomed company house, very tiny but decent enough for us to visit.

However, in 1975 our dad was transferred to a small train station called Melfort Station, where he just had a single room, so Mom could not take us to him anymore. He would come home for Christmas. Otherwise in between, Mom would visit him, with the baby. Those of us in school stayed behind with our grandmother, who had her own set of huts right next to ours.

My mom was always nursing a baby. She gave birth to twelve babies in the twenty-two years between 1957 and 1979. That's a new baby every other year. Ten of us survived to adulthood.

Mom made sure that she delivered all her babies in a hospital. Five of us were born in Salisbury General Hospital, the biggest hospital for blacks. She also kept track of all our immunization shots. Nobody ever missed those painful needles.

We had decent food. We never ran out of sugar, tea leaves, cooking oil, salt and laundry bars. I would say that's the whole grocery list. My mom produced the rest of the food in the small patch of land surrounding our home. She was able to fill up her grain storage room every year with maize. She also grew tomatoes, onions, sweet potatoes, peanuts and pumpkins.

Pumpkin leaves were a delicacy. They were cooked as a vegetable and served with maize meal (sadza). Most of the time we had our maize meal with kale or with cabbages. Sometimes we supplemented our diet with wild vegetables that grew abundantly in the rainy season – *Bonongwe*, *nhungumira* and *nyevhe* were the most common. Maize meal was the staple food, a thick porridge made out of powdered corn. On special days we slaughtered a hen or a rooster. We never fed these chickens. They just roamed about freely on the homestead, feeding on anything they could find, scraps of food from the garbage pit, worms, insects, frogs or snakes.

It was always exciting when Mom announced that we were having a rooster for dinner. We would hunt around the whole homestead to find the one that Mom had picked for the meal. All the children would start the big chase to catch the rooster. Sometimes it took up to an hour before anyone caught it. Then one of us would chop off its head with a sharp knife. If Mom was not watching, we would let go of it again, and giggle as the headless bird reeled around the yard for a few more seconds with a fountain of blood jetting out of its neck.

For bigger gatherings we slaughtered a goat. That was done by older men while young boys watched to learn the skill. Bulls were slaughtered for big gatherings such as weddings and funerals. Otherwise we raised cattle to pull the plough, to milk the cows, and to sell to the butcher's shop if we needed cash. I've heard people say that villagers in Africa survive on a dollar a day. That did not apply to any village I knew. We lived off the land, and it gave us plenty. There was no monetary value to our lifestyle. It was priceless.

My mother's name was Laura but the Shona accent had corrupted it to Rora, and that's how it appeared on all her identity documents. She was a full-figured voluptuous and curvaceous woman. In short, she was a typical African beauty. She had high self-esteem. She walked tall, and was usually in a jovial mood. Her smile exposed a wide tooth gap in her front jaw that was considered a beauty mark in a woman.

She never sat idle. If she was not working in the field, she was cooking food for us or breastfeeding the baby. When she finally sat down, she always picked up her knitting needles. She knitted all our sweaters by hand. She also had a hand sewing machine. She would collect scrap pieces of cloth thrown out from the textile companies in Salisbury when she visited our dad. Then she pieced them together to make us dresses that had small patches in all shapes, sizes, colours and textures. Those dresses were horrible to say the least.

To keep the witches at bay, Mom prayed profusely every morning and at bedtime. She took us to the Anglican church every Sunday. She was the leader of the women's league.

Church services were interesting. They were officiated by the deacon, Mr. Mbona, who was also our headmaster. Technically, the Sunday services were supposed to last for an hour, but they lasted for three hours, sometimes four.

Mr. Mbona was always punctual. He rang the loud church bell at ten o'clock, to signal the start of the service, but nobody was anywhere near the church yet. Some were still down at the river, taking their weekly baths. Others were ironing their Sunday best clothes.

Sometimes our deacon stared at the empty church pews for half an hour before anyone turned up. The church pews were two rows of long narrow plank benches with an aisle between them. The first person to sit on the bench had to be very careful to sit on the centre of it for balance. If he sat on one end, the other end was sure to swing upwards, causing him to slump unceremoniously onto the concrete floor. It was like a see-saw.

People trickled in slowly. By the time there were enough people to start the service, the hour had already passed.

The deacon was unfazed by that. He would take his revenge.

The only structured parts of his service were the beginning and the end.

"In the name of the Father, the Son and the Holy Spirit," he would start.

Then he would ramble on and on until everyone had dozed off. He would then start a hymn to wake them up, and then begin the sermon over again, or so it seemed, because everyone had totally lost the trend of it. By then the back benches would have gradually filled up with people who had arrived well after the sermon started. No one could tell what the theme of the sermon was because by the end of it all, our deacon had touched on every book of the Bible from Genesis to Revelations. After talking to himself for another hour, he would eventually utter the word that everyone was waiting for.

"Amen!"

Those who happened to be awake made sure to wake up their family members. A hymn would wake up the rest, as the congregation filed out of church. On the way out, it was not surprising to bump into a family that was just arriving at the church door.

Occasionally the white priest, Father Woodrow, drove the two hours from St. Augustine's Mission to celebrate mass with us. Those were special occasions and everyone was punctual. For this priest, one hour was one hour. He started mass at ten o'clock sharp.

"In the name of the Father, the Son and the Holy Spirit," he began.

He stuttered through his prepared sermon in our language. Nobody heard a word of what he said because of his gross mispronunciation of words that totally distorted the sermon. After the homily, he conducted the rest of the mass rituals strictly, making surreptitious glances at his wrist watch every now and then. At eleven o'clock sharp he said,

"Amen."

Then people gathered outside the church to greet each other. By then, Father Woodraw was already driving across the river, to the next village church where another congregation was waiting for mass. Tough luck to those had who missed the Holy Communion. Next time, they would be punctual.

By the time I did my fourth grade (1975), Clara, the first born in my family had stopped going to school. She ended in the seventh grade because of the educational system of the time. There were limited spaces for secondary education and so competition was very stiff. If kids did not pass the seventh grade national standardized test well enough to get a spot in secondary school, that was the end of their schooling. They were not allowed to repeat the grade. Passing meant getting 'A' grades in all subjects. That's how my sister missed the opportunity to get a decent education.

The second born was my brother Cybert, who was then fifteen and doing his Form 2 (second year in secondary school) at St Faith, Anglican Mission School in Rusape. It was a boarding school. The third born, Justin, was at this time doing seventh grade at Manunure school. It was in a different village, twelve kilometres away from ours. Every morning he had to climb the steep Mukunda Mountain to get there, but he was never alone. Those who had passed fifth grade in our community school, climbed up that mountain with him.

Climbing up the mountain was a daunting task. One had to crawl on all fours, holding on to the rocks, trees or the big roots that had been exposed by soil erosion. It was a good two hour climb if you were a vibrant teenager. If you were a middle-aged man or woman it would take you three hours, and if you were a senior, it was an impossible task. Coming down was interesting. The mountain was so steep that the gravitational pull forced you to run down it. Therefore, you had to make sure you looked ahead and marked a tree or rock that you were going to hold on to, to stop your acceleration, otherwise you would continue tumbling down, lose your balance and end in a nasty crash.

Many of the students who were supposed to climb up this mountain every day soon gave up, or just didn't bother to try it at all. So they never got an education beyond Grade 5. In my family, dropping school was not an option. Come hail come thunder, we had to go to school. My mom and dad were passionate about that. So both my brothers attended that school for two years before proceeding to boarding schools for their secondary education.

Neighbouring us were other members of the extended family. We had our uncles Giles and Cloud, who were younger than our father. They worked in Umtali and came home to their families every weekend. There was Uncle Robert, who was older than our dad. He stayed in the village. We also had our Aunt Stella, who had been widowed and had returned home with her five children. She stayed with our grandmother, with all her kids.

It was a big extended family. We had many cousins, but in our language there is no word for cousin, we were just brothers and sisters. On Christmas days, we all gathered for the annual feast. There were tons of bread baskets. Bread was spread with butter and a topping of red Sun Jam, a delicious mix of fruit, sweetness and colour. It was scrumptious. After that, we had rice and chicken. We ate the whole chicken including the head and feet. Nothing was wasted. We also got candy and cookies on these days if we were lucky. Every child got new clothes for Christmas. That was the Christmas present. We went to the Anglican church for the Christmas service.

Life was good indeed, but that was the calm before the storm. A dark cloud was hanging over us, and the fog was rolling in. A heavy storm was brewing, that would alter the rhythm of our community for ever.

THE STORM

One night in the middle of the rainy season of 1975, I was startled awake by a boom of thunder that rolled across our valley. Then came the heavy torrent of rain pounding against our corrugated iron roof. It sounded as if the sky was falling. The rain lashed down unforgivingly. I could hear the clatter of the corrugated iron sheets above us in the swirling wind that threatened to tear the roof apart. I peeked through the small window and saw the ominous black clouds that blocked the morning light, casting our village into a gloomy darkness. Every now and then lightning flickered, sending a brilliant light that blinded my eyes. I crawled back to lie beside my sister and covered my head with the rag.

I lay awake on the bamboo mat, wishing it was a weekend, but then, suddenly I felt the heavy rain pouring directly on us. I was startled. We all sprang out of bed, in panic. The roof was gone. We were exposed to the ruthless elements. The wind had ripped off the entire roof, crumpled it up, and deposited it about a hundred metres away from the house. We were drenched. Mom gathered us into the kitchen hut where she made a fire to warm us up.

The rain storm continued through the morning, but as usual Mom woke us up to go to school. There was no missing school under any circumstances. Slowly and reluctantly I opened my eyes, blinked, sat up, knelt down on all fours, stretched my arms up high, yawned, then I dragged myself to my feet and stumbled out through the door, leaving my two sisters Agnes and Elizabeth, still going through their own wake-up rituals.

As I followed Mom out, she suddenly fell to her knees, right in the middle of a deep, muddy puddle and under the pouring rain. She held her hands up, in a surrender posture, then she started clapping hands as if she was pleading for mercy. She mumbled something inaudible. There was horror in her eyes. It shocked me, and I froze in my tracks. What was it that had electrified my mother? Then I raised my eyes, and saw what she had seen. I trembled. I broke into a sweat. The other kids behind me stood transfixed to their spots as soon as they beheld the scene.

Camouflaged by the tall maize crop were three dark grim faces, bearing down on our mom. They were all pointing guns at her, or so it seemed. Guns! Guns! Guns, the scariest beasts of all time! More shadowy, rain drenched figures could be detected farther afield, partly hidden by the tall maize crop. Their horrific forms sent chills down my spine. I was paralyzed.

After what seemed like eternity, a voice came from a different direction, from someone we had not yet noticed.

"Don't worry, Mom", he said in a very gentle and reassuring voice. "Stand up and prepare your kids for school. We don't mean you any harm. We are your sons."

It took a moment for my horror-filled mother to register that this person was talking to her. In her mind she was probably already dead. Then the voice came again.

"I'm sorry if we startled you, Mom. Have you ever heard of freedom fighters?"

My mom must have realised who these soldiers were, for she stood up and looked relaxed, and they vanished into the corn field. It was all mysterious to us kids, but watching our mom relaxed and going about her morning routine as usual reassured us that we were safe. Everything was okay, we thought.

The rain storm slowly subsided as the sun peered from the eastern horizon, sending its crimson beams across the high mountains around us. Mom proceeded to get us off to school, but entreated us not to tell anyone what we had seen that morning.

That was our first face to face encounter with the Zimbabwe African National Liberation Army (ZANLA) forces fighting to liberate our country from colonial rule. It was a civil war, blacks against whites.

Apparently, under cover of the morning rain and fog, they had been able to make similar visitations to every household in the village. They had just come to make us aware of their presence in our midst.

That night they returned. They gathered us under a big fig tree, right in the middle of the bush. There they proceeded to politicise us, to educate us about the political history of our country.

They were fighting to free us from the scourge of the white man's rule, they said. Our country was supposed to be called Zimbabwe, which means stone house. It was not supposed to be called Rhodesia. It had been named after Cecil John Rhodes, a British imperialist who came to Africa in the 1890s, on a mission to conquer it and expand the British Empire. Our ancestors put up a resistance but failed to drive out the whites. The British fought with guns, while our ancestors fought back with spears, bows and arrows. It was an unfair match. They were massacred. The British settlers gradually increased in numbers and drove us off the arable lands to establish their own farms and plantations, while we got squished in the arid parts of the country, where rainfall was minimal and the soils were sun-baked and infertile.

Our people who had depended on cropping the land, could no longer produce enough food for their families, and were forced to work on the white man's farms and in their kitchens and gardens, where they were treated like slaves. Many more black people worked in industries and factories where they were paid meagre wages.

On the question of Christianity, our resistance fighters, told us that the British had tricked us by sending missionaries first. The missionaries gave us the Bible and told us to kneel down and close our eyes to pray. By the time we opened our eyes, our land was gone, stolen by the colonial settlers.

They told us that since time immemorial, our people had always worshipped *Mwari Musiki* (God the Creator). The only difference was that we worshipped him through our ancestors, but the whites wanted us to worship him through their own ancestors, the so-called saints. They talked about Saint Peter, Saint Paul, Saint Matthew and others. Of all the saints in their religion none of them were from the African continent.

They encouraged us to worship God through Nehanda, and Kaguvi, our ancestors who were executed by whites for leading the first resistance against colonial rule, back in the 1890s. Those were our saints, who died for believing in us.

That made a lot of sense to me.

Our soldiers urged us to unite against the whites. Now was the time to reclaim our birthright, to take back our land and our dignity. It was time for the African sons and daughters to unite against the oppressor. We all had a duty to play in this struggle: men, women and children.

I listened with a keen interest to this bush history curriculum I couldn't have heard in the classroom. They pointed out that Christopher Columbus did not discover America. There were Native Americans who lived there, who discovered it centuries before him. In our own country, David Livingstone did not discover the natural wonder that he named after his queen, the Victoria Falls. He was obviously shown this wonder by the local people who had lived along the Zambezi river for decades. Instead of studying a history that was foreign, distorted and irrelevant to us, it was time to make our own history.

It was an eye opener. I began to see things a little differently. Life was not as good as I had thought. In our prescribed school curriculum we were taught that before the coming of the white man there were warrior kings – Lobengula, Mzilikazi, Shaka and Soshangane – whose mission was to invade each other and steal each other's women and livestock. The white settlers had helped to pacify them and to stabilize the region.

They did not tell us that they were the real invaders. They did not tell us that they had stolen our land. They did not tell us that they used us as cheap labour, as they mined our gold, silver and diamonds and shipped the proceeds to Britain. They did not tell us they raped our women who worked in their kitchens, thereby creating a whole new race of people, the mixed race, which we call coloureds. They did not tell us that the white people, who were only ten per cent of the population, owned ninety per cent of the arable land in our country.

The freedom fighters pointed out to us children, that our school was a piece of junk compared to white children's schools in our country. Theirs were built under British standards, with libraries, cafeterias, large classrooms, big windows and tons of stationary. They had telephones and electricity as well as offices, secretaries and janitors. They had inside toilets with toilet seats and flush water systems. They didn't have latrines that could swallow live goats whole. The money that funded those white schools came from our soil, our gold, copper, tin, and diamonds as well as from our farmland. Our school had no electricity, no phone, no office nor secretary. I had to ask for the definition of the word janitor. I had never heard of it, for in our school, children had duty roasters to clean the classrooms, and the latrine, and to cut the grass.

Our soldiers travelled in troops of six or seven. They would spend a day or less camped in the bush outside the village, to get food supplies and get laundry done, then they would move on and another group would arrive.

They walked long distances at night, taking shelter in caves, ditches and under the canopy of thick forests.

They did not use their real names. They made up their own names that were their mission statements, and they preferred the title, Comrade.

- † Comrade Zvichanaka Munyika (All will be well in this country)

- † Comrade Tichafara Taitora (We will rejoice when we take it back)

- † Comrade Tichatonga Nyika (We will rule the country)

- † Comrade Rusununguko (Liberty)

- † Comrade Pfumo Reropa (Bloody Spear)

- † Comrade Nyika Yedu (Our Country)

- † Comrade Hondo Kuparadza (War is destruction)

Their midnight campaigns continued regularly. There was no age limit. My mom took turns with my aunts to babysit younger kids. They would gather all the children in one hut and leave one adult at home. We were not forced to go but it was fun there, and besides, if an adult missed two or three meetings people would start getting suspicious.

"Are you with us or against us?" That was the question they would have to answer, and no one wanted to be asked that question.

The freedom fighters were fully charged and emotional. It was contagious. We joined them in singing war cries, political songs and slogans.

"Forward with the liberation struggle!" they would shout.

"Forward!" we would all respond in unison, waving our clenched right hand fists.

"Forward with African unity'!"

"Forward!" we chanted, enthusiastically and emotionally.

"Down with colonialism."

"Down!"

"Down with whites!"

"Down!"

Oh how we fell in love with these soldiers! They spoke to our hearts and to our souls.

Their training and weapons were donated by China and Russia, with the help of Mozambique, and a few other African countries. Our freedom fighters had no paycheck at the end of the month. They were volunteers, entirely dependent on the villagers. Teenage girls did the laundry for them and cooked food, which they snuck into the bushes to feed our soldiers. At this time my sister Clara, the first born in our family was a teenager. She joined that rank of teenage female helpers, called *Chimbwidos*.

I visited them several times in the bush camp with my older sister. They never huddled in one spot. They were always scattered about the bush, shifting from one foot to another, ever ready with finger on the trigger. But they were happy people, cracking jokes, laughing and playing music or singing their revolutionary songs. There was never a dull moment there. They loved to see us children. After all, they were fighting for our future. Some of them had left young families at home so they loved to see us and could sometimes sit down on a rock in the bush to play a little game.

Teenage boys contributed by being the secret agents, (Mujibhas), finding information about the whereabouts of the Rhodesian army, so that the freedom fighters would ambush them. Many of the Mujibhas ended up sneaking into Mozambique to become soldiers themselves. Many young men and boys disappeared secretly at night without notifying their parents. Our famous drummer, Lameck was one of the many who left our village that way. We never heard from them during the war as they were always deployed to fight in other parts of the country.

Mothers provided the food, donating their cornmeal, eggs, hens and goats that were slaughtered for the meals served in the bush. My mother was part of that category.

Our soldiers did not have an army uniform. They just wore any dark colours that could camouflage them in the forests and hills. Fathers provided clothing, jackets, sweaters, shirts, and boots. It was indeed a people's army.

Meanwhile, the war was raging on in other areas throughout the country. It was a guerilla war, or a bush war. Our soldiers had no vehicles or aircraft, so they did not make a large scale entry into urban centres, but they did get close enough to throw their fire at some targets in the cities. They hid behind the bushes and ambushed the Rhodesian army trucks as they passed by. Sometimes they planted land mines on the roads, to blow up the trucks, and they could shoot down helicopters and jets. They had the advantage of knowing their terrain better than the white army. They also had the important advantage of support from the surrounding villagers like us.

Their army headquarters was in the neighbouring country, Mozambique, which had just won its own fight for independence from Portugal, and was helping us to liberate ourselves too. Our soldiers walked from Mozambique for hours and days, through the forests and hills, penetrating deep into our country to fight. Our village was very close to the border, and our terrain was very ideal for the bush war so we saw a lot of action there. Honde Valley is a very rugged terrain that is bounded on both sides by a system of hills and high mountains sloping down towards the Honde River.

Often we heard gunshots in the distance. Sometimes we saw swarms of helicopters and jets passing above our village on a mission to drop bombs in a mountain or valley where freedom fighters were spotted. Sometimes they were crossing over into Mozambique to bomb our refugee camps there or to attack our soldiers on their bases. Often, the encounters happened closer to the villages and unfortunate villagers were caught in the crossfire.

One Monday morning as we converged for morning assembly at school, one popular teacher was visibly missing. The headmaster later visited each classroom individually to break the sad news. A bus had been blown up by a land mine. Mr. Mupeti had perished in it. He had been travelling back to school from a weekend visit with his young family, which lived in another village an hour's bus ride away.

We were devastated. The whole class fell silent for a while as the news sank in. Then the emotions gradually gripped us. We wept bitterly. First, silent tears rolled down our cheeks, then there were muffled sobs. Then it was outright wailing. Some students turned to hug each other. Others fell to the floor moaning in agony. We were disconsolate. Similar cries could be heard in every classroom. The whole school turned into a grieving scene. We lamented our beloved teacher, the best teacher in the world. He unleashed the potential in us. He inspired me.

The land mine that killed our teacher had actually been planted by our own army. They had intended to blow up a Rhodesian army truck, but the bus got there first.

Similar loses of innocent civilians were reported in other villages surrounding us and throughout the country. The reports were all by word of mouth. Our freedom fighters had a tiny wireless radio in the bush but after the history lessons I had learnt in the bush, the propaganda on the Rhodesian news station was painful to listen to. Our soldiers were referred to as terrorists, communists, guerillas, rebels, insurgents, and other despicable terms. How could they be terrorists? They were only fighting for what rightfully belonged to them. Instead, we tuned in to the Radio Mozambique station. There we listened to slogans, songs and motivational speeches from the commanders in the army bases in Mozambique, but we were advised to keep the volume very low, for that radio station was forbidden by the Rhodesian government. Anybody caught listening to that station risked his life.

Many teenage girls feeding the fighters in the bush were often caught in the crossfire and massacred. We heard the scary story of seven girls killed in a raid in the Mandeya village. This village was farther east of us, close to the Mozambique border. We heard numerous accounts of teenage boys suffering the same fate while helping out as spies. Meanwhile my sister continued to help in the bush with others. One day we returned from school and Mom told us that she had sent Clara away to seek refuge in Salisbury. We were not to tell anyone. My mom had been worrying about her more and more as the war intensified.

Life had changed in our village. We could no longer play in the river. We were no longer allowed to be out at night. There was no more roaming the forests freely to collect wild fruit and herbs. Even our livestock could no longer forage freely in the dry season. The number of students attending school was dwindling. There were no more sports events, no more sliding in the stream, no more boxing matches in the river bed, and no more weddings.

My brother Justin was then in a boarding school at Marist Brothers Catholic Mission. It was a two-hour bus ride away from home. Our older brother was in Form 3 in a different secondary boarding school. They only came home for the school holidays in April, August and December. Our father continued to work and to send money to us and to the two boys, for their school fees. To him, there was no stopping school. It was his obsession.

Although the fear of death was overwhelming, life had to go on. Parents continued to dart into the forests to collect firewood, and to go down to the well to fetch water. They continued to work in the fields, and to take livestock out to graze. We still had to eat. A few of us continued to go to school.

One Saturday in January of 1977, my mom sent Agnes and me with small packages of dried maize, to the grinding mill, where our maize would be ground into the powder we used to make our staple meal, sadza. We joined two other girls going on the same mission. Balancing our loads on our heads, we trudged on, silently in single file, barefooted, on the hot, rocky, narrow path. Beads of sweat trickled down our faces, but we were not paying any attention to that. Fear enveloped us all the time. That was the new normal feeling.

Birds were chirping, squirrels squealing and there was a horde of different types of insects in the long grass, singing a collective chorus that formed the background sound of this hot summer day. For these creatures, life was still normal, but not for us. On bygone days we would have stopped to challenge each other to identify the various critters that made this music of nature, but not anymore. In the tall dry grass we used to hunt for grasshoppers and roast them at home for a crunchy snack, but not anymore. There was no more playfulness. We just wanted to accomplish our mission as quickly as possible. The sooner we came back home the better.

The sun was ablaze, above our heads. There was not even the slightest wind, so it was scorching hot. A huge vulture flew high up in the sky above us. In this wartime period, the myth was that a vulture flying high without flapping its wings was a bad omen. It signified a battle, but we saw vultures all the time, so it was hard to distinguish which one heralded danger.

Just outside the village, in a wooded area, we came across the horror of horrors: white soldiers.

They must have seen us coming and had hidden in the bush to startle us. That was cruel. We all stood there frozen like statues, totally dumbfounded and numb. Two white soldiers towered over us with cold stares, pointing their guns at us. After what seemed like ages, without a word spoken, one soldier approached us.

"Where are the terrorists? Where are the guerillas?" he barked. I flinched at his thick nasal voice. We stared at him in silence. He assumed that we didn't understand English so he decided to translate his words into Shona.

"*Magandanga arikupi?*" His pronunciation of the words was funny but this was no time for humour.

"We don't know them! We don't know them!" We all answered simultaneously with trembling voices.

They probably knew that we were lying, but we were just little kids so they told us to proceed to the grinding mill.

They had underestimated us. We were soldiers too. There was no way we were going to proceed to the grinding mill while they entered the village to attack. Our soldiers were there, and they needed to be warned. So we pretended to go on, but as soon as we were out of their sight, we dumped our loads in the bush and made a U-turn through the forest. We knew every nook and cranny of that forest. We had made all the paths that mapped it with our own bare feet. We sprinted back home to tell. It was the fastest I've ever run in my life.

We told the first adult we saw. Word quickly got relayed to our soldiers who were camped in the bushes behind our cattle pens. Our soldiers cordoned off the Rhodesians in the bush just before they entered the village. What followed was a massacre.

Gunshots boomed in rapid succession at different pitches. More gunshots cracked in the air like thunder. The noise was echoed in the surrounding hills and over the mountains, each loud bang imparting a degree of fear that I had never known before. After a brief pause we heard more isolated shots.

"Bang!" then again, "Bang! Bang!" Then there was silence.

We had arrived home just about ten minutes before the battle started, and we had told our mother what we had seen and reported. She did not get enough time to prepare a response to the sound of battle so close to home. She scuttled in and out of the hut several times, with all five of us following her in and out, like a train. Mom was so shaken that she didn't know whether to go out or stay in, run or hide. The fear in my mother's eyes caused me to panic. My imagination began to add its own horrors. What if the Rhodesians set our hut on fire? What if their jets and helicopters came and bombed our whole village?

Mom eventually settled for staying inside. We all huddled around her on the floor, waiting for destiny to take its course.

After a brief silence we heard the rumbling approach of helicopters flying low. They circled the whole village several times, then their sounds subsided and there was silence. The whole incident lasted just over half an hour but it felt like the whole day.

That night, we did not venture out of the hut. My mom always had some food available, as everyone else did in these war times. Our soldiers had advised parents to keep food available just in case. In a world where refrigerators were unknown, and the options of non-perishable foods were limited, we had bananas, mangoes, and peanuts for supper that night.

The next morning held horrors of its own. We could hear the pitter-patter of a light drizzle on our corrugated iron sheets that roofed our house. Since it was a Sunday, Mom wouldn't wake us up early. When I was pulling up the rag to cover my head for a little more sleep we heard heavy knocks at the door, countless booms in quick succession.

"Boom! Boom! Boom! Boom!" Somebody was obviously losing his patience, and before our mom had the time to decide what to do, the door flung open, falling, off its hinges. Two Rhodesian soldiers burst in upon us. One of them was a black man.

"Get up! Hurry up! Where are they?" yelled the black man in our own language. He was pointing a gun at my mom, while the white man started searching the room. It was a bare room except for the six precious souls that called it a bedroom. We were all lined up on the bamboo mat, all six of us including our mom who had started sharing our bedroom with us. Nevertheless, they picked up all those rags that covered us and threw them aside. Everyone was wide awake and scared to death.

"Where are the terrorists I say?" He was furious.

"I don't know," muttered my mother in a shaky voice.

"Don't lie to me like that. Do I look like a fool?" he roared.

My mother could only stare at the floor. By then, we had all bundled up behind our mother's back, staring helplessly at the soldiers. The white soldier who was doing the search went into the cooking hut. We heard the rattle of our pots and plates being kicked. Was he expecting to find a terrorist hiding in a pot? After making a big mess in that hut he came back to get his colleague and they zipped out to continue their search in other people's huts. It puzzled me that there was a black man fighting on the wrong side of the colour bar. What was he thinking?

We stayed huddled in that bundle for a while longer. Then Mom told us that it was okay. We could go back to sleep. But we could not sleep. In my state of fear my mind fabricated its own horrors that kept me giddy. I thought I heard footsteps outside, but there was nobody. Then there was a light knock on the door. But no, I had imagined that too.

The whole village was besieged that morning. The Rhodesians searched every hut, dragging out all teenage boys and young men. They herded them at gun point, to the army trucks that took them to Ruda Base Camp about half an hour away. Ruda Base Camp was a scare those days. Just the mere mention of it made people cringe. It was the centre for torture in our region. Rhodesians beat them up with the butts of their guns all the way there, and on arrival they tortured them some more.

When we came out of the room, it was raining more heavily. A light fog had enveloped the whole valley and a heavy wind had picked up. It was probably already midday and we were beginning to feel the pangs of hunger. We helped Mom to pick up the metal pots and plates that had been tossed out of the hut and were scattered throughout the homestead. Mom made cornmeal porridge for us.

While we were having our porridge we heard wailing in our neighbour's homestead. Two or three women started it, and more voices joined in. There was no mistaking that kind of wailing. Everyone knew what it meant. Somebody had died.

Our neighbours, the Nyamarebvu family had lost their grandmother in the battle. She had not come home the previous evening, and they had just found her body in the field where she had been working that afternoon.

Farther up the village we heard more wailing in a different homestead. The Musarira family lost their grandfather, who was caught in the crossfire while he was herding cattle.

It was a dark day indeed. The whole village was grieving.

That day Mom suddenly felt ill. She left us all with our grandmother and walked five kilometres to the only clinic that was still operating. She did not return home that evening. A message was relayed back to us from the clinic that she had had to board the bus to go to Umtali General Hospital for a medical emergency. That scared me but my grandmother did not seem to be too worried about it, so I took the cue from her and calmed down.

My grandmother's name was *Rusiya* (Lucia). Nobody knew her date of birth but considering that her first child was born in 1926, I can assume that Grandma was born around 1906. That would put her at the age of seventy-one, in the year under discussion.

Grandma Rusiya was illiterate. The only thing she could read was The Holy Bible and she read it fluently and thoroughly. When she was babysitting us she took that opportunity to tell us Bible stories. One day, when she asked me to read a letter to her, I asked why she couldn't read letters and yet she read the Bible. She explained that she never went to school. She had been taught to read the Bible in adult catechism classes at St. Augustine's Mission by the white missionaries. She had mastered the skill so well that she went on to teach Sunday school and catechism classes for many years at that mission.

Grandma prayed every morning and night without fail. Her prayers were long. When she started her bedtime prayer I always fell asleep before she finished.

She was a very well-built woman, with a firm body that made her look younger than her age. She had no wrinkles at all, but her skin colour was very dark, blackened by many years of exposure to the scorching sun while she worked in the fields. In my memory of her I see her in the field behind her hut, with a hoe in hand, weeding her maize crop. Year in and year out, that was her life. Apart from that, her other responsibility was to relieve her four daughters-in-law of the task of looking after the children. She was very loving and gentle with us. When I was old enough, I helped her to look after my younger siblings when our mom left us in her care.

After about two or three weeks our mother came back from the hospital. I noticed right away that she had lost a lot of weight, but wait, what was that she was holding in her arms, wrapped up in a blue shawl? Yes, that explained her dramatic weight loss. She had a new bundle of joy, her ninth baby.

We quickly crowded around to welcome the new member of the family, but when I took a peek at him, I had questions. I had seen new babies before but this one was different. It was a scrawny little thing with wrinkled skin that seemed to be dangling off the bones. The tiny eyes hardly opened at all, and the cry was a very feeble, distant whimper. *Surely something is wrong with this baby,* I thought.

Then I heard Mom explain to other adults who came to see her new baby. On the 3rd of February 1977, my mom delivered twin boys prematurely at six months. One of them did not make it through the night. The other one was this pitiful looking tiny one. Mom also said she had not been alone. She had got in touch with our uncle who worked in Umtali, and he had been a great help, visiting her at the hospital every single day. Therefore she named the baby after him, Cloud Farai.

Mom also had good news for us. While she was in Umtali she had been able to talk to our dad on the phone. He had finally been granted a transfer from the tiny train station, to a small town called Banket. There, he had a four-roomed house, so we were all going to live with him.

After all, we were no longer going to school. All schools in Honde Valley had closed down. In 1977, I was supposed to climb up the mountain to attend Grade 6. I don't regret that the war saved me from that ordeal.

Mom was going to wait for the baby to gain a little weight because he was too small to travel long distances on the crowded buses. By the time he was two months old, Farai had turned into a big bouncing healthy baby.

During the April school holidays of 1977, Justin came home for the school holidays. He was fifteen. He was to travel with us all to Banket, to our dad. Mom needed an extra hand with all the little ones. Our older brother Cybert was seventeen and could not come home anymore. Home was too dangerous for boys of his age.

The afternoon before our scheduled departure there was a sudden rumble of helicopters, and a fighter jet flying low towards our village. It seemed as if someone had sold out our soldiers' base because the aircraft went directly there for the kill. Everything happened fast. They dropped bombs whose deafening explosions sent tremors all around. The cacophony of flying aircraft, and the explosions created a scene from hell. It was a continuous assault.

We all rushed into the hut for cover. Mom watched through a small window to see what was happening outside. We heard her repeat, "Oh my God! Oh my God! Oh finish!" She was panicky.

She had seen several huts ablaze. Meanwhile, explosions continued. Assuming that the Rhodesians were going to torch every hut, she decided to take us out into the open. That split second decision she made that day saved our lives. Our hut immediately burst into flames.

We all lay bare on the ground, in the sweltering heat, watching the huge flames lick up the dry grass and poles that had been our roof for many years. Even the baby did not make a sound. Meanwhile, a helicopter circled above us so low that it raised a cloud of dust that blinded us all. The dust and the smoke, plus the scorching heat of the sun, as well as the rumbling helicopter all at once created a horror scene beyond description.

Eventually the sounds of the helicopters receded beyond the mountains and everything went silent. Mom went over to Grandmother's hut to check on her. She was crouched behind the door, praying, too scared to move.

The whole event had taken just a few hours, but it felt like a whole day. My mom feared most for Justin, who was home for the school holidays. If the soldiers came back to search the village for any wounded freedom fighters, and to interrogate people as they always did after an event like this, my brother would be targeted.

So my mother retrieved a piece of crumpled up cloth hidden in her shirt. She unwrapped it, and a wad of ten dollar notes dropped out. Mom took out one ten dollar note and handed it to my brother.

"Here, take this and go," commanded my mom firmly.

"Where to, Mom?" asked Justin, totally confused.

"Just go! Go! Go!" insisted Mom.

My brother sensed the urgency in Mom's voice and hesitantly took the money, but he didn't know what to do. Where did Mom expect him to go at this hour? The sun was setting and a battle had just occurred out there. He was scared. He looked at our grandmother, searching for her opinion, but she was too shaken to say a word.

"Go Justin. I said go!" Mom was agitated and impatient.

Reluctantly Justin walked out, closed the door behind him, and left. He was wearing a dirty khaki shirt and shorts, with a crumbled ten dollar note in his pocket.

For a long time that evening we continued to hear helicopters circling the village and landing every now and then. More explosions were heard in the Mukunda Mountain.

The death toll of our comrades that day remains unknown. The Rhodesian army always picked up the bodies to burn them up or to bury them all in mass graves, so there was no way for us to tell how many were killed or if any of them survived. It was a group of seven very vibrant young men devoted to their cause.

The village also suffered more casualties in this battle. A woman from the Makahamadze family perished in a fire. Two mujibhas who were in the bush with our soldiers at that time also perished.

Mom could not turn her back on the grieving families. She had to wait until they were buried.

But the carnage of that week was not over yet. Another group of Comrades came into our village. They were furious. Three of our own villagers were suspected of being traitors. They were accused of selling out our base. Some people claimed to have seen them in the helicopters. There was no investigation for concrete evidence. It was instant justice. They were sentenced to death. They were led into a thick forest. Adults were summoned to come and witness the horror so that they dare not commit the same crime. The three suspects were chopped up with machetes and their bodies were left for scavenger animals to feed on.

I knew one of the men very well. Makoto was just a village clown who made everyone laugh. His clown name was Makuru Scope (Cool Scope). It never made sense to me that he was accused of such a heinous crime. Some villagers were settling their personal vendettas with their enemies by making false allegations against them to the Comrades. In a neighbouring village across the river, three people had been locked up in a hut and burnt alive because they were suspected to be witches. Similar incidents were happening throughout the country.

At the time Makuru Scope was being savaged, we were herding cattle with his son, Evison. Everyone in the village knew what was happening and boys were teasing him about it. That was brutal to a kid who already suffered merciless teasing every day because he had one eye. We called him Evy Zisorimwe (One-eyed Evy). The nickname was so commonly used that it sounded like his last name.

About a week after all this rollercoaster in our village things had calmed down a little, but a rumour was beginning to spread in the village, that my mom and dad were deserters too. They were wondering why our dad didn't come home anymore. He wasn't contributing enough to the struggle. Why did our parents continue sending their sons to boarding schools while other people's sons went to war? Nobody else in the village was attending school at this time. We were at war.

If this rumour gathered momentum, my mom could suffer the same fate as Makuru Scope. There was no more time to waste.

Mom was woken up by the first cock crow. Our aunties helped her to take us all to the bus stop before dawn, to board the bus to Umtali. We had to walk in small groups of two or three because a large group attracted suspicion from the Rhodesian soldiers, and we didn't know who to trust among our fellow villagers. My mom usually didn't show any signs of anxiety but on this day I saw a hint of fear in her eyes. Would we make it to the bus stop, which was beyond the steep Mukunda Mountain?

Meanwhile I wondered. Where was Justin?

MOTHER DUCK AND
HER DUCKLINGS

That journey we made, to Banket, fleeing from our war-torn village has stayed vivid in my memory.

In those days we always travelled between Umtali and Salisbury by train, using a free train pass that we had because our dad worked for the company. It was an overnight trip. The train left Umtali at 9:00 p.m. and arrived in Salisbury at 7:00 a.m. It was slow business. (The distance between the two cities is actually about 270 km, a three hour drive.)

We arrived in Umtali at 8:00 a.m. It was a cloudy morning with a persistent light drizzle. Where was Mom going to keep us for the layover time of over twelve hours before boarding the train at 9:00 p.m.?

That was not a big problem. Our Uncle Giles worked in Umtali. We would go to his house, spend the day, have a hot lunch, play outside, have a delicious supper, probably take a shower, and then go to the train station.

That sounds simple enough, but here was the complication.

Our uncle worked as a cook and gardener for a white family in the affluent white suburb of Yeovil. Black people were not allowed there, except of course the cooks, nannies and gardeners, but there was no way our mother was going to spend twelve hours with us in the blazing heat in the Africans' waiting room at the train station. She was taking us there anyway.

On her head Mom balanced an old brown suitcase. Strapped to her back was baby Farai. Her left hand held the tiny fingers of four-year-old Rudo, and her right hand held six-year-old Abigail's little hand. Behind her, and holding on to her skirt were three other scared little squirrels, Elizabeth, (eight,) Agnes (ten) and me (twelve).

Such was the scenario as she navigated her way through the traffic. Her plan was to board a taxi to take us into the white suburb. There was no way a black woman could walk through those streets with a train of babies like that without exciting the dogs and causing a stir.

The taxi dropped us by the cemetery. From there we followed a back alley towards the white man's mansion. It was tough for Mom to manoeuvre us that short distance as we were stunned by the magnificence of that property. We were hypnotised by it. It was beyond anything we'd ever imagined, but we had been cautioned not to make any sound, not even a sniffle or sneeze, or else guard dogs would be set on us. So we held our silence and trotted close behind our mom.

We snuck into the yard through the small gate at the back yard that was meant for the black workers. They were not allowed to enter through the front gate. Right there by the corner of the yard, inches from the barbed wire fence, and facing the back alley, was the dilapidated little brick cottage that was the cook's house. The whites referred to this outhouse as the boy *skia*. Regardless of age, all the African house workers were regarded as boys or girls, so our uncle, who was over forty years old, was the garden boy. There was no lock on the door of the boy skia, only a rusty wire that my mom unlatched, and she drove us in. We had made it undetected.

Uncle did not know that we were coming. The only possible means of communication would have been a letter, but because of the war, the postal service to rural areas had stopped. So this was an ambush. We waited.

It was a tiny cluttered room with white walls that were yearning for a new coat of paint. There was a single spring bed in the centre. On it were a few old rags for blankets, a few dirty socks, a cook's white apron and a few khaki shirts and shorts that were his work uniform. Apparently, the bed was also the wardrobe. The only other place he kept clothes was a big cardboard box that was under the bed. In the corner was a Primus stove, a burner fueled with kerosene. Next to it was another cardboard box with two small metal pots, two plates and a cup. Another box had a quarter of a loaf of brown bread, a can of jam, a knife, a box of Tanganda Tea, a kilogram bag of brown sugar and nothing else.

So there was no hot breakfast here. There was no food. My mom took out the cooked sweet potatoes and pumpkins she had packed in our luggage from the village. They were starting to get slimy and a little stinky, but we devoured them.

We had to go around the building to get to the toilet, which was attached to the cottage. Inside was a squat hole, much like the ones in the village, except this one had plumbing connected to the master's house. Our uncle could flush the toilet, and if he closed the squat hole with a heavy metal lid, he could stand on top of that and take a shower. Well it wasn't really a shower. There was no shower head, only a rusty metal tap pouring from above.

After midday, uncle came home for his lunch break. He walked in and:

Peek-a-boo! The room was full of little people on and under the bed and in every corner. Mom was sitting on the floor. It was a pleasant surprise.

"How did you do this?" He was smiling from ear to ear. Happy to see us but wondering how Mom had managed to get in there with a whole litter without being detected. Uncle was holding a plastic bag with leftovers from his master's table. That was supposed to be his lunch, scraps of fried chicken wings, rice, potatoes and bread crumbs. He shared that among us and returned to work.

Once we had eaten the lunch we became a little restless. We were not used to such confinement. Our mom allowed us to take turns to stand on the bed and look out through the small window that was way up there.

There was a vast luxuriant garden that stretched as far as my eyes could see. It was covered with a carpet of luscious green lawn. It was a mini forest, strewn with all manner of flower bushes in full bloom. I was able to label only a few that I had learnt about in the plant unit in Mr. Mupeti's class: roses, marigold, petunia, daffodil, and bougainvillea. I had never seen most of these in real life, only in magazine pictures he showed us.

Amidst the lush green lawn stood a huge house that was beyond description even though I could only see the back view of it. It was a two storey stone building in shades of brown and black. The numerous windows were huge. The green gabled roof sloped to both sides. Again, I had only seen such houses in magazine pictures.

In the far end, there was a playground, with swings, slides, and a see-saw, all painted in bright primary colours of red, yellow and blue. I had only seen such things in pictures. Our teacher had been very good about bringing the outside world to us through reading books to us and showing us pictures of things that were beyond our imaginations. The only swings we had played on were the ones we improvised on a tree brunches. Quite often our swings broke and we went home with bumps and bruises. Wow these were real swings, how I wished I could get to try them just for a minute.

Then I saw two blonde girls just about my age walking from the house to play on the swings. A little toddler followed behind them kicking a ball, a real soccer ball, not a paper one like the ones we manufactured back home, with plastic bags and rugs bundled up and tied up with sisal rope. Behind them all was their nanny, wearing her work uniform, a blue tunic dress with a matching apron and a hat. Both girls sat on the see-saw while the nanny pushed the little boy on a swing. I watched them with so much envy that silent tears just streamed down my eyes. Mom pulled me off the window.

"What's wrong?" she asked. I did not answer. How could I tell my mom that I was crying because I envied white kids playing on swings? I just pretended to rub my eyes as if they were itchy.

Next to take a peek was my little four-year-old sister Rudo. It seems her eyes did not notice anything else out there besides the playground. She immediately broke into tears.

"There is a playground," she sobbed, "I wish I could go on the swing." She voiced my thoughts.

"You have to turn into a white person first, before you can go on a swing like that!" snapped my mom. I don't know whether that made any sense to the little child, but she was silenced.

In the evening, uncle came back with another package of leftovers. He probably cooked more food on purpose, so he could sneak out enough food for us. We binged on it.

We returned the same way we had arrived. Since it was getting dark and the vicious guard dog had been let loose, our uncle had to lure it into the dog kennel, lock it up, then let us out of his house. Behind the cemetery, we boarded a taxi that took us to the train station. Our uncle came along with us.

At the train station we huddled around our mom in the crowded, mosquito-infested African waiting room, which was a large open hall with dirty white walls. There were two rows of wooden benches that soon filled up and latecomers sat on the hard concrete floor.

Boarding the train was quite dramatic. There were too many other passengers like us, fleeing their war-torn villages. It was a stampede. Our uncle fought his way in first, then my mom handed him the three youngest of us through the window. He held the seats for us while Mom struggled in with us three bigger kids. She heaved a sigh of relief when she eventually slumped into the seat. Then uncle went back to his cottage, and we were on our own again. Meanwhile, more and more passengers continued to pile in. The seats had long since filled up and people were standing in the narrow aisle, holding on to the rusty metal railings. They only stopped crowding in when the train rolled off the station.

The interior of the Africans-only carriage was anything but luxurious. There were two rows of hard plastic seats, in a light green colour that was dulled with dirt. It was hot, stuffy and noisy in there. There were arguments and some minor skirmishes every now and then. Everyone seemed to be grumpy. Mom begged people around her to allow us to sleep under their seats. We couldn't sit up all night. She guarded over us until we arrived in Salisbury early in the morning. By the time we arrived in Salisbury the floor was a smelly garbage heap, with banana and orange peels all over the place.

From the Salisbury Train Station, we walked to the Charge Office where we boarded the city transit buses operated by the Salisbury United Omnibus company.

They were off-white, with a red line. I liked those buses. They were decent and we passed many of them as we drove to Harare Musika, the long distance bus terminal (now Mbare.)

Boarding the bus at Harare bus terminal was another ordeal similar to the one we had encountered when boarding the train. There was overcrowding and chaos. The luggage being loaded on the rooftop of the bus was in itself a summary of the pandemonium. There was a medley of items including sofas, beds, wardrobes, wheelbarrows, baskets and of course numerous suitcases and bags in all shapes and sizes.

Somehow we eventually ended up sitting on the bus. We didn't actually sit on the bus. Mom was holding baby Farai and the rest of us sat on the laps of strangers. Although I was twelve years of age, I was too small for my age so no one could guess that I was already a pre-teen.

My exhausted mom dozed off as the bus cruised down the Mapinga Pass. It had been two full days without sleeping a wink, and the last few months had been a rollercoaster. Now she could relax. At least this was the last lap of our long journey to Banket.

On the drive from Salisbury to Banket, I noticed the absence of hills and mountains. The terrain was very different from what we were used to in Honde Valley. It was all flat land. There were large lush green fields stretching as far as my eyes could see, and no huts in sight. I guessed, from the history curriculum I had learnt in the bush, that these must be the white men's farms. This must be the fertile land they had stolen from us.

Banket was a farming town. The most noticeable landmark there the rows of about twenty giant cylindrical towers shooting up into the sky. Mom told us that the tall towers were the grain silos where the commercial farmers stored grain for local markets and for export. Behind the silos was a cotton ginnery, and then there was the railway station, where my dad worked as a clerk. There was no passenger train there, only freight trains that transported farm produce from the surrounding farms. Across the train tracks, there was the whites-only residential area. Our bus turned in the opposite direction, into the narrow street that led to the dusty African residential area.

Today I remember this journey, not just as a physical journey, but also as an intellectual and emotional one. I was growing up.

PICTURES

Mom and Dad with baby Abigail

(left to right) Elizabeth, Mom with baby Rudo and Abigail

FROM THE FRYING PAN INTO THE FIRE

Mom

Mom and her sister Naomi

Dad

(Left to right) Clara, Cybert, Uncle Giles, Judith and Agnes

FROM THE FRYING PAN INTO THE FIRE

(Left to right) Mom, Aunt Stella with baby Judith

BANKET TOWN

Banket was a whole new chapter in our lives.

When we arrived, our dad was at work. It was a small town. We just asked at the bus terminal, for directions to the Railway Workers' houses. It was not far.

The door was not locked. Mom opened the rusty brown door and there was somebody inside.

"It's Justin! It's Justin!" we all shrieked.

Justin had arrived a week before. We were overjoyed to see him.

We had all suffered silently, not daring to pester Mom about him, and she had hidden her concern from us.

He recounted to us his ordeal of the day he left home. Since Mom had given him money, he had guessed that Mom just wanted him to board a bus and go anywhere away from danger. It was evening time though and buses to Umtali were only available in the early morning. Anyway, he just decided to go up the mountain in the direction of the bus stop. The helicopters and fighter jets were buzzing overhead.

At the foot of the mountain he met an elderly woman, Mbuya Masasa, who was scuttling down the mountain in fear. The battle had started when she was at the mountain top, collecting firewood.

She motioned him to follow her, and she took him to her home. He spent the night there with her children. The next morning she disguised him in a little girl's skirt, and he climbed up the mountain to catch the bus. Ten dollars was enough money to get to Banket.

After musing about Justin a few minutes we all went about exploring our new home. Well that took only a few seconds because there wasn't much to it: four small rooms that were barely furnished. There was a living room with three old couches, a kitchen with no appliances, a bedroom for our parents and a bedroom for us all.

Our dad came home in the evening, bringing with him on his bicycle, some bamboo mats and blankets for our bedroom.

"Baba! Baba! Baba! Dad! Dad! Dad!" We all chanted excitedly when he arrived, all of us crowding around him and hugging his long legs.

"Oh! Oh! Oh! Crowd! Crowd!" He beamed happily as he lightly tapped each little head. "Ok! Ok! Now go outside and play," he said. Then he picked up the new baby whom he was meeting for the first time. He held him at arms' length as he usually did with babies, and as soon as the little one started twisting his little limbs and making those ugly faces that babies make to signal that they are uncomfortable with a stranger, Dad handed him back to Mom.

"Here take him back. He is crying," he said. My dad just didn't cuddle babies.

The day after our arrival Mother took us to school. Kuwadzana Public School was right next to our house but she wanted us to go to St. George's Roman Catholic School, which was the only other school in the town. Although we were Anglican, Mom said any Christian education is better than no religion at all. However, it turned out that both schools were already full. Many families had also fled from the villages surrounding the small town, so there were no vacancies left.

Our dad was heartbroken by that when he came home from work that day.

"How do I say I'm a father when I have kids who do not go to school?" he said. Our dad believed that education our licence to liberty. That day he did not go to the beerhall.

No one had a TV. There were no toys except what we improvised ourselves. We made our own balls from plastic bags filled with rags and tied round and round with rope. We made our skipping ropes by tying pieces of rags together. There was nowhere to play except in the dusty streets. When other kids came back from school we joined them to play. The streets were packed with kids playing soccer, netball, skipping rope or hopscotch. One of us had to stand aside as a sentinel to watch out for approaching cars, then he would call out to others to get off the road. The cars would zip past us at top speed, raising a cloud of red dust that would blind us all for a minute. Then we would resume the game. By the time we went home for supper we were all covered in dust.

Our sister Clara was like the second mother to us all. She did all the cooking, always making sure that everybody was present for the meals. We ate from the same plate, so our meal times were always an eating contest – who could gobble down the most food the fastest. Of course the winner was always Agnes. We always cleaned out the plate and asked for more. Our sister would scratch the bottom of the pot really loud. That was her way to announce that there was no more food.

Our sister was a clean freak, always scrubbing the walls, mopping the floors, and handwashing our blankets and clothes that were always dyed with the red earth. When we returned from our street games she was always blocking the doorway to prevent us from coming in. We had to take a cold bath first. The bathroom, which was also the toilet was attached to the house but had a separate entrance. There was no toilet seat, no flush water system and no shower. There was a large squat hole that was obviously not made with children in mind because it was too wide for small kids to squat astride. So my little siblings under seven had to use a toilet pot and then dump the shit into the squat hole. There was no indoor water tap in the house. There was one communal tap to every six houses. We collected water in buckets, for all our needs, including watering down the toilet. To take a shower we closed the squat hole with a lid then we brought in a bowl or a bucket with bath water.

On Sundays, we went to the Anglican Church with Mom. It was a small building not much different from the one in our village. There were similar benches inside too. There was a deacon called Mr. Muringani, who conducted the Sunday services. Once every month Father Sinclair came to conduct mass. I asked Mom where Father Sinclair went to church every Sunday, and she said there was another Anglican Church in the white suburb. Mom said we were allowed to go there but she would have to ask Father Sinclair first, or else we would startle his white congregation if we suddenly walked in unannounced. So one day Mom did inform the priest that she was bringing her family to his church.

We got to the cathedral early and we all sat huddled in the corner. It was a big building, beautiful inside and out. The church pews had heavy oak wood benches with back supports and padded kneeling pads. There were all kinds of white statues of Jesus, Mary and Joseph. I thought God really was for whites when I saw these statues, but I dared not say that to my mother.

The white people visibly cringed the moment they saw us. They sat away from us, across the aisle. A few adults politely grinned at us. We were fascinated by the beautifully dressed little kids, but they were visibly scared of us.

I did not like the service at all. The singing was horribly dull. There was none of that funfair we had in our black church where the hymns were accompanied by the African drum and various kinds of rattles. We responded to the rhythm of music by swaying our bodies or waving our arms. In our lively church it was impossible to stay still like statues as these white people did. They really looked bored.

After church there was tea and biscuits. We never had such a luxury in our African church so I liked that part. Mom told us to wait until all the whites had lined up first. Their little ones were just staring at us. Mom later explained to us that some of them had probably never sat under the same roof with black children. They only interacted with black adults who worked in their homes as nannies and gardeners. Besides having their own churches, whites had their own hospitals and schools. For shopping they went to the City of Salisbury, where blacks were not allowed in certain shops. If a black was sent shopping there by his boss he had to do so through a latch in the back wall of the shop.

Dad did not go to church. His argument was that God was not for black people. Whites were the ones who had everything to thank him for.

While we were gone to church Dad used to make his favourite dish for us. He bought offal, cow lungs, and tripe from the butchery. He mixed those with large chunks of tomatoes, onions and kale, then he boiled everything together. The side dish was always the usual sadza. We always looked forward to that dish when we got home from church.

I was just beginning to know my dad. Until then, I didn't know him very well. He was just this guy we visited in Salisbury for four weeks once a year, the guy who usually came home for Christmas, bringing us clothes and lots of bread and meat. Other than that there was no emotional attachment.

He was a tall handsome guy with an athletic body and a bald head. He must have become bald in his thirties because he was always bald, as far back as I could remember. As soon as he got home from work he took a shower and left for the beerhall. That was his daily undisturbed routine, but he was not an alcoholic. He basically went to socialise with his large circle of friends, and to share news about what was happening around the country. He always gave Mom the whole paycheque at the end of the month, then he would beg for a dollar every day to go to the beerhall. Mom was responsible for the family budget. We never missed a meal. None of us was ever sent back home from school because of unpaid fees.

The dollar was enough for Dad to buy one packet of cigarettes and one mug of beer, just enough to make him a little tipsy and more talkative. He spoke with a very loud booming voice. I sometimes wondered if he was a little deaf because he spoke out loud even when he was supposed to whisper.

He usually came home from the beerhall before we went to bed, and that was time for a family history lesson that he told us over and over again, with a passion. He always started the lesson by proudly introducing himself:

"Ndini Taengwa mwana waRusiya. Kufa kwangu zvarowa! My name is Taengwa, son of Lucia. My death will be the end of an era!"

He punctuated his lecture with these same words over and over again. It was like a chorus.

Dad was born in 1929. He was the second born to Lucia and Sydney Mawoko. Sydney died early, leaving my grandma with three young children: Robert, Nathan and Giles. However, according to our traditional culture, if a man died, his young widow did not need to look elsewhere for a husband. She had to pick one of his younger brothers. So my grandma picked Justin who already had a wife, but that didn't matter. His wife had no say in it.

So Justin fathered two more babies with my grandma. Those were Stella and Cloud. Our grandmother would never have told us this detail for fear of divisions within her family, but our dad spilled the secret to us when he was drunk.

Dad told us that the Mawokos used to live together as an extended family in the Penhalonga area. That's where he spent his early childhood and attended school. He was very intelligent and his mother struggled to pay his school fees, raising money by selling peanuts and brewing beer. She eventually gave up, leaving my dad still yearning for an education. Education was the dream that he desired to fulfil through his own children, but he revered his mother for the effort she had made for his education.

In 1930, the colonial government had passed the Land Apportionment Act, which divided up the whole country along racial lines, giving the fertile lands to the whites to establish their farms and plantations, while blacks were driven to the less desirable parts of the country. When that law finally caught up with his community, they were forced to leave. The whole family tree was uprooted, and its branches scattered throughout the country: Murehwa, Marondera, Rusape and Nyanga. My grandmother's second husband moved to Chirarwe Village in Mutasa. My grandma and her children settled in Honde Valley.

Urban areas were designated for whites only. Blacks could only be there if they could produce proof of employment in the form of a town pass. My dad's little education landed him a clerical position with Rhodesia Railways. Dad married my mom in 1957 and they had their first child Clara, the same year. Back then, he said the company provided one room for the man only. Women and children were not allowed in the city, so Mom stayed in the village and tilled the land. My dad was later transferred to the capital City of Salisbury, which was a two day trip away from Mom.

My dad never spanked children, but his words stung. His worst moments were when somebody brought home a bad school report. He would lecture us on and on. Mom spanked only the little ones when they were being whiny and annoying, not too sure what they wanted. She would slap their buttocks to give them a good reason to cry and go to sleep. Once we were old enough to go to school we were not spanked. They talked to us. If we misbehaved in the presence of a visitor or in a public place Mom just gave us a look that spoke volumes. We would quit immediately without a word spoken.

We soon got bored with the town life. The routine was too limited. We woke up late. We had our morning skirmishes over household chores, and then we waited for other kids to come back from school so that we could play with them in the street. We missed our village life, our school, our sliding, our swimming and our free roaming in the forests looking for wild fruits. We even missed our goats and cows, and the bee and wasp stings. One day we came home with a wonderful idea. We surprised our mom with it.

"Mom we found a job!" we said. Our mom just kept a straight face as if she didn't notice our excitement.

"Well tell me about it." She thought we were joking.

We were twelve, ten and eight. But age didn't matter. Other kids were working and their employers had encouraged them to bring more friends. Mom couldn't say no. After all she also needed a little break from our noisy chatter, so she allowed us to go to work.

The next Monday, we went to work with our friends when they returned from school. Schools dismissed at 1:00 p.m. every day, so there was plenty of time to work. We boarded a tractor in front of Banket Beerhall. It was overloaded with kids, a few sitting passengers and most standing. Each of us was holding the tool of the trade, a hoe. We were going to weed in the soya bean field at Nicolle's farm. Many other tractors belonging to white farmers around the town converged at that point to collect children to work on their farms.

Our drive to work was hilarious. We sang and cheered for the tractor driver to increase speed, but the squeaky old machine could only go up to thirty kilometers per hour. When we were dropped off, the mood changed. It was serious business. The supervisor explained that it was a dollar an acre. If we weeded an acre he would record our names and pay us on Friday. We had no concept of the size of an acre so we maintained our composure, until he actually finished measuring our acres by counting his strides. We were shocked. Each acre was about the size of a football field. The three of us decided to work together on one acre. By the end of the day we were exhausted but still hadn't finished it. Our friends, who were more experienced, finished theirs and came to help us, and we recorded our acre for the day.

The drive back was not so exciting. Nobody sang. We were sweaty, itchy, tired and hungry. Nicolle's farm was large. There were lush green fields of maize, tobacco and soya beans, receding as far as the eyes could see. We could fall asleep, wake up, fall asleep and wake up again and still be on Nicolle's farm. The rest of the week we came every day but we were less ambitious. It took us two days to finish weeding an acre. The work was tough but when we got paid it was always exciting. We put our coins together in a tin can that we used as a piggy bank. We wanted to fill it up first, then share our savings.

We continued working until one day our mom heard that a tractor had overturned on another farm and kids had been injured. So she stopped us working. After sharing our coins, Elizabeth used her money to buy sweets and chocolates. Agnes and I wanted to use our money wisely. We had seen some pink bikinis through the shop window at Gorvan's Trading Store, so we went shopping there. However our money was not enough for two bikinis, so we put our savings back together and bought one big parachute underwear for our mom.

After that our dad found a better job for us. He had planted a vegetable garden along the railway tracks near his workplace. There were beds of cabbages, rape, onions and tomatoes. There was a tap nearby, where we could fetch water for the plants. Initially we used buckets but later he bought a hosepipe. A few other neighbours also had gardens there. We were able to produce enough vegetables for our family and there was even surplus to sell. The selling was the tricky part because the market was flooded. We had to wake up very early in the morning to fill up our baskets with bundles of the leafy greens and go door to door, selling the bundles for five cents each. We kept this occupation for a long time.

One day towards the end of 1977, we got home from our work and found our parents very unhappy. Dad was not preparing to go to the beerhall. They had sad news about our village.

"You know what girls, Kwambana village is no more," said our mom. We stopped eating and stared at Mom, too scared to ask for an elaboration on that.

She explained that all the people had been herded out of their homes without notice. They had been placed behind a barbed wire fence, ten kilometres away from our village.

"Concentration camps! Concentration camps!" my dad kept saying. I didn't understand what he meant by that.

Anyway what had actually happened was that the Rhodesian army had decided to cage villagers throughout the country, to prevent them from helping the freedom fighters. Each Protected Village or Keep held a few thousand people from several different villages. It was made up of a wire mesh, with barbed wires at the top. Landmines were planted around the fence to prevent people from coming in and out other than through the single gate that was manned by the Rhodesian guard forces. On the international news they reported that the Rhodesian army had established Protected Villages to save the civilians from carnage by the marauding insurgents. The real motive was quite different. We called them Keeps. Their purpose was to keep the villagers out of touch with the freedom fighters in order to starve them.

A few days later we arrived home to find Mom gone. She had had to go back to Honde Valley to bury her mother Grandma Judith. She died suddenly in Ngarura Keep, which was not very far away from ours. The death toll in the Keeps was high because many people failed to cope with the appalling living conditions.

The following year, when things had settled down a little in the Keep, Mom, Justin and I went to the village to check on Grandma Lucia and the rest of the extended family. The crowded and filthy conditions in the Keep were evident the moment we entered the gate. There were some pole and mud huts roughly put together in a hurry, most so low that adults had to crawl into them. Since our villagers had been moved during the rainy season, they had suffered untold hardships, carrying their belongings and walking ten kilometres in pouring rain. They were allowed to go outside the fence to cut down trees and grass to make their shelters. Each time they entered or exited the gate they were thoroughly searched to make sure they were not taking out food or bringing in anything suspicious. There was a tap water point where people fetched water in buckets, but food was not provided. They still had to walk the ten kilometres every day to grow crops on their fields. A six- to-six curfew was imposed. Anyone who missed that curfew was presumed to be a terrorist and would be shot.

At the beginning of the new school year, in January 1978, we were enrolled in St. George's Catholic School, Banket. There were four of us. Abigail (Grade 1), Elizabeth (Grade 3) Agnes (Grade 5) and I was in Grade 6.

School was good, but not as dramatic as our village school. I came top of the class most of the time. I had become brighter than ever before.

The following year, our oldest brother Cybert enrolled in a technical college in Salisbury, to study for a diploma in mechanical engineering. However a few months into the course our parents received news that he was in jail. Now what crime had he committed?

His crime: he had been called up along with many other college students, to join the Rhodesian forces, to fight against the insurgents, and he had missed the deadline to report for national duty.

From jail, he was sent for army training. That was a very difficult time for my parents. How could they tell people that they had a son fighting on the wrong side of the war? That was just unthinkable.

That year our mom went to the hospital again. She came back holding a new bundle of joy draped in pink woolens. Then there were ten of us. My dad was not the kind to analyse little babies, but I overhead him say to Mom, "You are getting better at this every time. This one is the cutest of them all." That was true, Tsitsi Bridget was indeed a gorgeous little doll.

INDEPENDENCE

The whites eventually gave up the fight. On April 18, 1980, we celebrated independence from colonial rule. The joy was overwhelming. The country's name was changed from Rhodesia to Zimbabwe. Umtali became Mutare. Salisbury became Harare, and many other names of towns and roads were changed too.

Robert Gabriel Mugabe was the new leader of the country. He preached reconciliation between blacks and whites. All schools, hospitals and other segregated facilities were open to everybody. Many whites could not bear this. The thought of spending a day under the same roof with black people was unimaginable to them. They could not tolerate such humiliation, so they emigrated from the country in large numbers. Some moved into our neighbouring country, which was still ruled by whites, South Africa, where the system of racial segregation was even more clearly defined and thoroughly enforced. Others returned to their roots in Europe.

Many white farmers remained and continued their business as usual.

My brother Cybert went back to complete his diploma in mechanical engineering. Justin got a scholarship to study civil engineering in Italy and I went to St. David's Bonda boarding school. From there I went to the University of Zimbabwe. My younger sisters did not have to go far from home to get a secondary education. Hundreds of schools mushroomed throughout the country. Colleges filled up and expanded to accommodate so many people who had been denied an education. The majority of my siblings went to teachers' colleges.

People could buy or build houses wherever they could afford. Our father bought a stand and built a decent four bedroomed house with a proper plumbing system, water and electricity.

Back home in Honde Valley people returned from the Keep, and slowly rebuilt their homes. My mother started rebuilding in a new location, just about a kilometre away from the original homestead.

I visited the village in those early days after independence. The whole atmosphere in the village had changed drastically. It seemed that adults had forgotten how to smile, and children had forgotten how to play. Many families suffered heartbreaks when they waited for days and weeks, for their sons to return, but many of those who went to war never came back.

Lameck, our famous drummer was one of the few who returned. I was excited when I saw him from a distance. I was going to ask him to play the drum one more time. Maybe he could restore the rhythm of our village. Maybe he could bring back the laughter. When I got closer to him I noticed that he had lost one hand. His right arm had been amputated just below the elbow. That broke my heart. You need two hands to beat the African drum.

That enchanting drumbeat was never to be heard again in our village. The rhythm of my village was indeed altered forever, and for the whole country, another storm was brewing.

CRY THE BELOVED COUNTRY

When I was a university student I met the man of my dreams. He was a real life fantasy. He was a graduate accountant, working in the university where I was a student. I was totally enchanted by him. I smelled him even when he wasn't with me. His voice rang consistently in my ears even in my sleep. I saw him ahead of me and behind me wherever I went. I felt the touch of his hands all the time and all over me. To say I was in love is an understatement. I was bewitched.

He was captivated by me too. He told me everything a woman wants to hear. I was angelic; I was his goddess. He was dazzled by my smile. I was his sunshine. We were soulmates. We were two peas in a pod.

We were just right for each other. There was nothing to wait for. He had a good job so he could support me while I finished my bachelor's degree. So we went ahead and introduced each other to our relatives and friends, and before long, we had said our marriage vows. For better or for worse, in sickness and in health, we would always have each other. It was a dream come true. Or was it really?

When I was in my second grade I asked my mother why I didn't have a Shona name. All my siblings had an English name and a Shona one but mine were both English, Judith Irene, "Why is that, Mom?" I asked.

My mom laughed, then said, "You had one that your grandmother gave you but you wouldn't want to hear it."

She then went on to say the name, and my young sister who was always too close to me like my own shadow overhead that name and burst out laughing. It was a long name, in fact two full sentences combined. Agnes teased me about that name for a long time. *Tozivascihatipedzimaya.*

Yes, Mom was right. I didn't want to hear it. It sounded like mumbo-jumbo, a gush of meaningless sounds.

It was not until I was a university student that I began to wonder what my grandmother had meant by that name so I asked her when I visited her back home in Honde Valley.

She told me that the name had been an expression of her own disappointments at the time she named me. Before I was born my mother had lost a day-old son. Her other two daughters-in-law had been losing babies and having stillbirths and miscarriages, and so the question was, how do we know that this one will survive? How do we know? (*Toziva sei?*)

We never get enough time with them. (*Hatipedzi maya*). My grandmother went on to tell me about her beloved late husband Sydney. He was taken when she thought life was just beginning. She never got enough of him and life was never the same again.

My Shona name assumed a personal meaning for me on December 26, 1987. Thomas and I had visited his parents in Mutare for Christmas. Thomas woke me up in the morning and said he was feeling very thirsty and dizzy. I went to get him some water to drink. Then he said he wasn't feeling well at all. He needed to go to the hospital. He died at noon that day. He was only twenty-seven. I was twenty-two years old, and seven months pregnant. It was an anticlimax.

If I could shed tears of blood, I would have cried them that day. It was as if the ground had suddenly slipped from under my feet. All my hopes were suddenly shattered to pieces. Those castles we had built in the air suddenly came crumbling down. We were going to do our masters degrees. We were going to buy a house in Borrowdale Brook. He was going to buy me a Mercedes Benz. We would have three children. They would all go to the best schools in the country. We would fly to the Caribbean islands every year for vacations. He would never leave me, no matter what.

As I stared down at his still body in the coffin, in that eerie silence of death, I just wanted to ask him one question.

"Why?"

I pinched myself several times. Was this for real or was it just a nightmare? To say I was disappointed is an understatement. I was distraught. I was angry. What did I do to deserve that? Why me? I felt stripped of any future I had ever imagined. I was disconsolate.

The day I gave birth I cried afresh. How was I supposed to balance the joy of birth with the grief of death? How was I to watch her take her first breath and not remember how he breathed his last? When I saw other fathers holding their newborn babies, kissing them, and analysing their delicate little limbs, I cried some more. I had never felt so lonely in my life. I wanted to share the joy of parenthood. Of course my loving mom was there. My very supportive mother-in-law was there too. But it was not the same. I wanted somebody else to be sitting where they were sitting. Even they felt the same way. They were trying to be brave, just for my sake, but they were distressed too. I could see that in their eyes. I cried a river.

My mother-in-law was the first to pick up the baby. She smiled, but there was pain in that smile. How do you pick up your very first grandchild and not cry, knowing that she will never be able to say "Me and my dad—Me and my dad," as little kids always say.

My love story mirrored the events in my country as a whole. Zimbabwe was quickly becoming a country of shattered dreams, broken promises, deaths, despair and tears. Our brief romance with independence soon faded away. It was a betrayal.

To write about the story of Zimbabwe after independence is like rewriting the book, *Animal Farm*. In this book, George Orwell describes the road from revolution to tyranny in a way that strikingly resembles what happened to my country in recent years. There was a great chasm between the genuineness of the war of liberation and the psychopathic greed with which our leaders destroyed our economy. Heroes of the liberation struggle became the vicious, tyrants who brutalized the citizens they fought to liberate. They said they cared about us but they scared us.

In *Animal Farm,* the pigs led a revolt against the human masters. All animals were equal. Everyone had a part to play in the revolution. They were united beyond measure. They spoke the same language, sang the same songs, and some died for the worthy cause. When the humans were overthrown, the pigs slowly got consumed by corruption and greed. They started oppressing their fellow animals just the same way they were oppressed by the humans. Pigs gradually evolved into human beings themselves. They moved into the farmer's house. They even started wearing dresses, and eventually they were walking on two legs.

In the late 1990s, President Mugabe decided to redistribute land back to blacks, in response to mounting pressure from subsistence farmers who were heavily congested on small patches of land.

This land reform program was a very noble idea considering that the dispossession of our people by British settlers had been the fundamental reason for the liberation struggle. The land question had remained an unresolved issue. For another twenty years, white farmers still possessed the bulk of the land.

However the whole process of land redistribution was marred by corruption and greed. Government officials grabbed the biggest farms and farmhouses from the whites, leaving many peasant farmers in villages still landless. Some top officials, including our president himself, grabbed three or four farms for themselves. Other people who applied for land had to be members of the ruling party. If they were known to belong to any other political party their applications were turned down. Some of the land officers demanded bribes in order to process the applications. Many of the poor people who really needed land had nothing to offer in terms of bribes, so they got nothing.

Not much was produced on the farms given to blacks. They had no farming equipment and they had no access to loans to start up the farming business. The result was chaos on the farms and starvation in the country. The country that was once the bread basket of Southern Africa became a land of beggars.

Meanwhile, the trend of corruption and greed infiltrated every organization. In the year 2000, I could not find a spot in a decent secondary school for my daughter although she had passed primary school with 'A' grades. I needed to pay a bribe to the headmaster, or a series of bribes before I even got the application forms.

There was nowhere to report crimes because the police force had become the most corrupt organization. People could commit any crime as long as they were able to bribe the police officers to shut up about their cases. Anybody aligned to the government was immune to prosecution and top government officials were invincible.

I could not drive in my homeland without being stopped by the police every ten kilometres, demanding a bribe. To drive from Harare to Honde Valley I needed to have extra cash to pay my bribes all the way. One day we were stopped by the police. They found no fault with our car. They found no fault with our identity documents, but they kept searching. Eventually they found fault with us having a camera in our car. They grabbed the camera and started analysing every picture we had taken. We had to pay a bribe to get the camera back or else we would spend the night there, and the risk of being savagely beaten up was very real. Citizens were more afraid of police officers than criminals.

Government ministers and top government officials were the most corrupt individuals. They stole money allocated to their ministries, and built luxurious palaces for themselves. The Minister of Home Affairs, built an insane fifty-bedroomed mansion for himself, while the majority of the citizens barely had a roof above their heads. Some paid themselves hefty salaries of forty thousand US dollars a month, leaving the employees without salaries, roads and bridges unrepaired, and schools and hospitals without supplies.

The government splurged millions of dollars on luxury cars for government officials – Range Rovers, Mercedes Benz sedans, and Land Cruisers – while the majority chugged along in privately owned, old commuter omni-buses that killed people by the dozens every month in accidents on the pot-holed roads. Meanwhile government officials siphoned the millions of dollars earned from dia-monds and other minerals, to their overseas bank accounts, while teachers and nurses went unpaid for months.

Water and electricity supplies went off for hours a day. Sometimes a whole week passed without a single drop of water coming out of the tap, forcing people to drink contaminated water from open wells. As a result there were several outbreaks of cholera over the years. Those who could afford it, dug boreholes on their properties in the city. Others had diesel powered generators to light up their homes, but very often there was no diesel at the gas stations. The majority made wood fires outside the houses, for all their cooking, and they lit up the houses with candles. While the whole world progressed in technology, we had gone backwards.

Robert Mugabe, whom we revered as our deliverer, during the liberation struggle soon turned into a merciless dictator, with secret agents and police hounds snarling at anyone who raised a voice of dissent. Many disappeared without a trace. Who ever heard of a ninety-three-year-old president? Only in my country.

Mugabe and his ministers seemed to think that they deserved it all because they fought the liberation war. Well the real heroes are the dead ones. What about those comrades whose bones still lay undiscovered in the caves and crevices of the mountains in Honde Valley? Where were their parents and brothers and sisters? They were among the millions who were unemployed, and homeless. The unemployment rate was estimated at ninety-five percent.

They were among those who got beaten up by party youths, the police and the army, in the run-up to the elections, to force them to vote for the ruling party.

They were among those who had suffered broken limbs in severe beatings from the savages in police uniform, during peaceful demonstrations. If they survived that torture, they left the country for the shanty towns of South

Africa, where they lived as refugees, in fear. They suffered xenophobic attacks by the South Africans, who accused them of congesting their job market. Many Zimbabweans were murdered with machetes in South Africa.

Mugabe and the government officials were convinced that they deserved to be the privileged elite because they were the liberation war heroes, but what about the unsung heroes like Lameck, who even lost an arm in the struggle? Didn't they deserve a share too? The last time I visited the village I saw him so drunk that he didn't seem to realise that he was at a funeral. Funerals are very solemn occasions in Honde Valley but Lameck was dancing to music in his head that nobody else could hear. He was twerking wildly and spinning his broken limb. He was beating an invisible drum. He was a broken man, both mentally and physically.

Our war veteran had become the joke of the village. Children did not even know his real name because the whole village called him Sigimbu (Broken). I had a little chat with him about the olden days, and he told me that if he had known what the future held, he would have chosen to continue beating the drum rather than going to war.

Yes they said liberation war heroes deserved it better, but what about me? That day I nearly broke my little legs running to inform the Comrades that the Rhodesian soldiers were approaching, I believe I fought this war too. Where was my reward? Where was my share of the national cake?

They said we were all soldiers. They said we were all equal participants in the struggle. They lied to us. We were betrayed.

Soon after independence a gravel road was constructed, right through my village, and we had buses passing through our village, so that we didn't have to climb up the mountain to get to the bus, but that was short-lived. The road was never maintained and it soon got overgrown with weeds. Life in my village went back to where it was in 1970, if not worse.

When I was in that bush in Honde Valley during the war, listening to Comrade Tichafara, (We shall rejoice) if someone had told me that I'd spend my adult life as a refugee in a foreign land, I'd have smacked him in the face. My family was scattered all over the world, along with millions of other Zimbabweans who were political and economic refugees in South Africa, Australia, Canada, India, China, the United Kingdom and numerous other countries. In 2008 a loaf of bread cost over ten million dollars. The inflation rate rose to over fifteen billion percent, and more people left the country.

Some people asked me why we didn't go back and fight for our rights. Nobody wanted a war. If you had seen what I saw in Honde Valley; if you had ever ducked a helicopter spitting fire, you wouldn't want a repeat of that experience. Whom would we fight anyway? The president owned the national army and the police force. Government officials lounged in their luxury mansions, and Mugabe flew around the world in national planes that had become his private property.

Some said go back home and fight through the ballot box. In 2007, Morgan Tsvangirai, the leader of the main opposition party, was brutally attached with iron bars by the police, leaving him with severe injuries. He went on to win the elections in 2008, but Mugabe refused to step down.

My country was a fake democracy. The people who cast their vote decided nothing. The decision was made by those who counted the vote. Vote rigging started right from the voter registration. The whole electoral process was a fraud.

Once upon a time my grandmother made a delicious dish for me but the dog stole it. Behind it was a trail of bones.

Once upon a time the freedom fighters fought for the resources in my country. The whole nation was puzzled by the mystery of the vanished wealth. Our government officials had plundered it. Behind them was a trail of million dollar mansions.

EPILOGUE

A week after writing the last chapter of my book, a dramatic event occurred in Zimbabwe that opened a new chapter in the history of my country. The Zimbabwe National Army, staged a coup d'état against Mugabe. Millions of Zimbabweans took to the streets to demonstrate their solidarity with the army.

I watched with mixed feelings, as these events unfolded. There was anxiety, excitement and apprehension when news of the coup broke out. Was this the start of a civil war?

I watched with pride and relief as millions of Zimbabweans marched peacefully in the cities on November 18th, 2017. The joy and feeling of togetherness was overwhelming. Thanks to technology, I was able to follow events live, on social media from thousands of kilometres away. I wished I had been there in person, to participate in this historical moment. On November 21st, 2017 Mugabe was forced to resign.

However, when I heard that Emmerson Mnangagwa, the vice president, was to be the new president, I became skeptical about the whole scenario. What exactly, were we celebrating? Was this a change at all? Was this a new start?

The new president, Emmerson Mnangagwa was a war veteran who fought side by side with Robert Mugabe during the liberation war. For the thirty-seven years that Mugabe had been in power, Mnangagwa was a top government official, hopscotching from one ministry to another, and eventually becoming the vice president of the country. He had about fifty years of total loyalty to Mugabe, and the ZANU PF party that destroyed our country. He benefited from the corrupt system and propped up Mugabe to stay in power. He had been a central player in the human rights abuses that characterised Mugabe's government. During the party rallies, Mnangagwa referred to the ZANU PF party as the sacred party that was entitled to rule Zimbabwe forever.

Was he going to change his whole ideology, that had been identical to that of his predecessor, or was he just a power hungry opportunist who had taken advantage of Mugabe's old age and frailty, to seize power from him?

The same argument could be made for Constantino Chiwenga, the army commander who led the coup. During the coup, he announced that the army was not taking over the government, but a few weeks after the coup, Chiwenga was sworn in as the new vice president of the country, and several top army officials became cabinet ministers. Chiwenga was a war veteran and a staunch supporter of the Zanu PF party. He had been in the national army since independence. He rose through the ranks until he became the army commander. Together with the national police force, the army has been part of the whole system that had propped up Mugabe for thirty-seven years. They shad been the instrument for intimidating and crushing the opposition parties.

The army had never been a custodian of constitutional rule and democracy. Rather, it had been the military wing of the ruling party. In 2008, when the opposition party won the election, the army commander, Chiwenga, vowed that he would not salute any president from another party, and the army unleashed a reign of terror against supporters of the opposition party. Many citizens bore scars of the horrendous acts of violence perpetrated by the army.

So was our national army commander genuinely shielding ordinary Zimbabweans, as he claimed, or was he simply shifting positions, to prop up a younger, and potentially more vicious tyrant?

Did they suddenly realise the human rights abuses that they themselves perpetrated, or were they shrewd connivers, giving themselves and the ZANU PF a new lease on life?

Mnangagwa immediately consolidated his power by appointing a new cabinet, but he picked the same old war veteran ministers who had served for decades under Mugabe. Essentially it was a military government, disguised as a civilian one.

While some people viewed this as the beginning of a new era, others considered it as the beginning of a new error.

ABOUT JUDITH

Debut author Judith Mawoko arrived in Canada from Zimbabwe in 2001. She had earned a Bachelor of Education and taught secondary school English for several years before immigrating. She now teaches in Alberta. She hopes her memoir will inspire readers to face life's challenges with hope, determination and resilience.